CHICAGO PUBLIC LIBRARY
HAROLD WASHINGTON LIBRARY CENTER

R0030279752

W9-BYC-371

REF   AUDIO-VISUAL CENTER
PN   Eliot, Marc.
1992.3
.U5   American
E38   television, the
cop 1   official art of
            the artificial

DATE		

AUDIO-VISUAL CENTER

FORM 125 M

REF
PN
1992.3
.U5
E38
cop.1

AUDIO VISUAL CENTER

The Chicago Public Library

Received 9-1-83

© THE BAKER & TAYLOR CO.

AMERICAN TELEVISION

Also by Marc Eliot

DEATH OF A REBEL

AMERICAN TELEVISION

THE OFFICIAL ART OF THE ARTIFICIAL

Marc Eliot

Anchor Press/Doubleday
Garden City, New York
1981

REF
PN
1992.3
.45
E38
c op. 1

The Anchor Press edition is the first publication of AMERICAN TELEVISION.
Anchor Press edition: 1981

Library of Congress Cataloging in Publication Data

Eliot, Marc.
  American television.

  Includes index.
  1. Television broadcasting—United States.
I. Title.
PN1992.3.U5E38   791.45′0973
ISBN 0-385-14953-0

AACR2

Library of Congress Catalog Card Number 79-8016
Copyright © 1981 by Marc Eliot
All Rights Reserved
Printed in the United States of America
First Edition

41/
R

To Jeffrey

ACKNOWLEDGMENTS

The question I heard most the past two years was "Why a book about television?" which only served to reinforce my conviction and commitment. Therefore, I now want to thank all who asked, even those who asked in disbelief.

It is impossible to thank everyone who helped me, directly or indirectly, along the way: those who added bits here and pieces, those who "found" episodes of shows previously thought "lost," those who pushed me to continue when I thought my ideas were turning to static, those who read sections still in progress and were willing to talk about them deep into the night, past sign-off.

David Herwitz provided fine legwork, in addition to assisting in some of the more tedious aspects of research. Charlie Priester's contributions during the middle writing stage were essential. I also want to thank Pat Wyatt and Rick Eaker for their assistance.

Jennie Anderson's contribution was very special. She shared my excitement and ideas, adding her special magic of love and embracing patience. She's also very funny.

I spent a year doing little more than watching television, part of that time at UCLA's incredibly well-kept TV archives. The staff were low-key, serious; devoted to preservation of television. I thank them for letting me come and go, roam through their inventory, seek their advice.

I'd also like to express my thanks to Mel Berger, Marie Brown and Laura Van Wormer.

This book really began when I was six years old. Having missed being admitted to kindergarten that year because I was born too late (April), according to the New York Public School System, I passed my time of day in front of our Zenith 21" watching the Army/McCarthy hearings, waiting for "Howdy Doody."

New York
May 17, 1981

CONTENTS

Playing solitaire till dawn
With a deck of fifty-one
Smokin' cigarettes and
Watchin' Captain Kangaroo
Now don't tell me
I've nothin' to do . . .

The Statler Brothers

ONE

The Official Art of the Artificial

I

Television is by far the most popular American entertainment medium; one of those things everyone does and everyone denies doing. Television has produced more than enough material to fill three major network schedules with new shows as well as hundreds of affiliate, independent and cable stations with a constant repertory of more than thirty years of well-preserved programing, still available to a greater or lesser degree, for broadcast. A quick flick of a switch in most major cities will offer several VHF and UHF channels, plus an ever-growing number of narrowcast cable and satellite systems, twenty-four hours a day, seven days a week, fifty-two weeks a year.

All one needs to watch television is a television (the term "television" being the signal being broadcast, the product contained within the signal, or the shows, as well as the technical equipment used to send and receive those signals). To this end, the awareness of technology and the subsequent participation in that technology by the viewer becomes an active, aggressive contribution to the experience of "watching television." Few theater-goers take into account the nature of the theater they attend when going to the movies, or the house a play is occupying when they go to the live theater. With Broadway shows, in particular, there is no choice on the part of the theatergoer in choosing one theater over another. With film and live theater such aspects as lighting, scenic design, projection clarity, and sound volume are "invisible," undetectable units at their most effective. However, the television signal and its subsequent reception depend heavily upon the viewer's participation, allowing him to assume a uniquely active role. A viewer chooses the brand as well as the type of TV receiver he prefers. Sony color or Zenith; large screen, big sound over small screen, poor sound. He adjusts his antenna or cable control box to achieve optimum reception. He manually adjusts color and tint, physically changes channels to program his nightly viewing. He adjusts sound, even turns the set on and off at will. Hopefully. Understanding and controlling the technical operation of his "set" is an important factor in his viewing experience. And yet, this aggressive technical participation is offset by the passive nature of the available programing.

His participation becomes an option which forgives the regiment of programing and its inherent lack of flexibility. Or, the plastics encourage aggressive participation while the abstracts encourage passive reception.

Form on television is simply not flexible. It is a predetermined constant, set physically even before the first glimmers of an idea have occurred. Television is filled with endless chunks of programing time: half-hour, hour-, and ninety-minute slots which must be filled. The requirements for filling these time segments are determined by advertising revenue, rather than artistic commitment. The structure of advertising on television—before, during, and after all programs—is rigid, a standardized pattern of content to "fit" structure. Through the years this structure has become ever more rigid; the "plastics" absolutely determined by advertising revenue. This is why films originally shown in movie theaters become "edited for television." They must conform to a predetermined format; usually two hours. Except for very unusual circumstances, a film will be "chopped" to satisfy its time slot with little regard for its "abstract" qualities, with total regard for the "plastic" nature of the work. Often a surrogate director will be assigned the role of manipulating the original director's vision, an act that all but dispenses with any notion of directorial "vision," inflicting a sense of conformity on a work that began as a creative act. Those moments removed from the original film are most often moments of violence, or sexually provocative scenes, or politically imflammatory situations. This is done to procure programing "more suitable" for the general viewing public. An example of this was the network showing of Arthur Penn's *Bonnie and Clyde*. All scenes suggesting Clyde's sexual impotence were removed, thereby destroying one of the most important explorations of his overly violent personality. The final, memorable climax, the explosive execution of Bonnie and Clyde, was so severely edited that the entire rhythm of the movie was destroyed, offering no release for the two hour build-up that originally preceded this "purging" of the violent, sexual, and political outlaws, the anti-"heros" of the film. Ironically, Bonnie and Clyde where "rehabilitated structurally, then executed.

The two prevailing influences within the commercial television industry are the corporate advertisers who control the flow of considerable revenues, and the federal government, principally but not exclusively through the auspices of the Federal Communications Commission. The advertising industry seeks wealth through effective repetitious hawking of its goods and services utilizing TV's method of reinforcement through complacency; a commercial for a product becoming a "hit" (and by extension the "quality" of the product rising in direct proportion to its recognizability) through sheer repetition. "Buy name brands" becomes a moral, as well as commercial guideline. The government seeks to maintain its position of power through the repetitious selling of name-brand law and order, the effective reiteration of a high standard of law-abiding morality. The abstract rejection of either the corporate or government "mainstream" would be, risky. Or, to put it another way, going out on a limb chances low ratings, risks cancellation and the probability of being replaced by something more acceptable, more popular, more repetitious, more complacent. A better brand.

Networks determine the success of its shows by ratings. High ratings are accepted as proof large numbers of viewers have watched or are watching a show. Continual high ratings define a "hit," a show that attains viewer status quo, a ritual of complacency.

How this process of complacency is maintained is best explored through an examination of television's programing; the external plastics of TV entertainment product as well as the internal structure, the abstract themes, points of view, and emotional effects that combine to reinforce the status quo rather than to question it, or change it.

One of the first places to avoid looking is where it might appear most logical to begin, the reporting of the news. The government and the corporations openly boast of their non-intervention in the free reporting of the day's events, openly embracing the unchecked liberties of the fourth estate. This is not to say there aren't problems with confidentiality, the public's right to know, equal time, equal coverage, slanting, ratings competitions, conflict of interest between sponsor and network, etc. These are problems which, by virtue of their presence suggest that news programs rather than being thorns in the official rosebush, are in fact the roses themselves, easily pointed to as evidence of a free and open communications society.

Nor should one look to the daily soap operas that reflect little more than a fluffy airing of housewives' fantasy, sex and violence reaching levels of empty excessiveness in order to balance the levels of empty excessiveness in housewives' real lives. The sheer repetitiousness of the characters and situations, no matter how spicy, are yet another form of relentless complacency, congratulating Mrs. America for being more complacent, than all those unhappy people living in a world where electronic organs signal danger.

Nor should one-time affairs such as mini-series be considered as representative of the structure of television. "Roots," the most popular mini-series of all time (and one of the most viewed programs in the history of television) has vanished from the networks, if not from the memory. Its obligatory sequel, "Roots II," didn't do nearly as well in the ratings, and most of the handful of mini-series that followed failed to attract as much viewer interest as the original "Roots" did. Little changed on television as a result of "Roots," either stylistically or in terms of programing and scheduling. Having served its revenue-producing and socially fashionable requirements, having ruptured the normal network schedule by its daily playoff scheduling, and having scored its hit-and-run ratings coup, it simply ceased to be; a peculiar aspect of its own existence.

The place to look is the prime-time network schedules themselves. This is where the action is, where the big advertising dollars are spent. The challenge for those working in television isn't to change the status quo through artistic revelation, but to produce programing that achieves a level of competence, efficiency, and emotional impact within the accepted limitations of structured complacency. Do the best of these programs achieve moments that, when studied within the context of their plastic and abstract qualities, in fact approach a level all the more provocative given their restrictive creative boundaries? Or, are they only illusions that shine more brightly because of the dullness of the competition; so carefully processed, so meticulously sanctioned they are not works of provocation at all but merely the transmission of this illusion, the official art of the artificial?

II

What is often referred to as "form" on television is actually "format"—a combination of genre (Western), length (one-hour Western), schedule (one-hour Western every Wednesday evening at eight o'clock Eastern, seven o'clock Central). A script for a half-hour television situation comedy must fit a format of twenty-two minutes and thirty-five seconds, with little, if any, allowable variation. The following represents an actual format outline requirement for a situation comedy that aired during the 1978 television season on the CBS network:

ACTUAL TIME	DESCRIPTION OF SEGMENT	SEGMENT TIME	CUMULATIVE TIME
9:00:00	Newsbreak	1:00:00	9:01:00
9:01:00	Open delay	:01	0:01:02
9:01:03	MAIN TITLES	:53	9:01:56
9:01:57	First commercial	1:03	9:02:00
9:02:01	ACT ONE	10:04	9:12:05
9:12:06	Second commercial	1:03	9:13:09
9:13:10	CBS Promo	:31	9:13:41
9:13:42	ACT TWO	12:33	9:26:14
9:26:15	Third commercial	1:03	9:27:18
9:27:19	CBS Promo	:21	9:27:40
9:27:41	CLOSING CREDITS	:29	9:27:59

The actual amount of time allowed for the presentation of this show was twenty-two minutes and thirty-seven seconds, excluding opening titles and closing credits. The remainder of the half hour was used for advertising and station promos, including a one-minute newsbreak.

Several years ago the FCC (Federal Communications Commission) adjusted the time allowed for commercial spots per hour as part of its continual regulation of the industry's practices. The effect of this slightly altered format indirectly changed the "look" of shows. It was most obvious in half-hour situation comedies with the demise of the one-minute pre-first-commercial "teaser" segment, and the thirty-second "epilogue." Imagine an episode of "All in the Family" having a sixty-second teaser before its first act, or a thirty-second epilogue ending with the whole family standing around laughing hysterically in the finest tradition of "Father Knows Best." The Bunker saga is simply inconceivable as we know it in that format. Archie's particular "problem" in any given episode was usually brought into the script almost as an afterthought, the first minutes devoted to something other than the main story line. The series often ended with a close-up, creating a moment different from the all-resolving family laugh. Format change leads to about content change. Conversely, repetitious format leads to repetitious content. This is another way of saying what people say about TV all the time, that everything on TV "looks alike."

This tightly controlled program structure conforms to an overall network program schedule. Each of the three major commercial networks—the Columbia Broadcasting System (CBS), the National Broadcasting Company (NBC), and the American Broadcasting Company (ABC)—begin and end their programs on the half-hour or hour. None of the networks risk viewer defection by changing this established structure. Together, the networks form a horizontal uniformity, so that the viewer is free to select an evening's schedule from all shows offered. In doing this there is passive cooperation among the networks, a respect for healthy competition along the wavelength borders.

If these concurrent network schedules can be regarded as "horizontal," the individual schedules of each network can be considered "vertical." The daily schedule of each network is the result of extensive planning, experimenting, and consecutive slotting to insure the highest individual and overall daily ratings. This vertical schedule is offered to the affiliate, or local membership station, which chooses from it the programs it will carry. The number of stations subscribing to a single program greatly affects the amount of money the network can charge advertisers for commercial time. The planning begins during the day as each network hurls game shows, soap operas, and talk shows at the audience, building momentum toward a combined commuter/ housewife contingency for the early-evening local news, usually beginning at five or six o'clock. These first newscasts are community oriented, utilizing an "eyewitness" concept of electronic journalism to create a heightened sense of audience identification with the community as much as with the individual reporter. Only occasionally does a major national or international story get indepth coverage by virtue of a network-feed pickup, the same way a local newspaper might rely on wire services for its national and international coverage. Local TV coverage of "big" stories is mostly headline material, with the promise for details to come on the national, or network, news, usually immediately following the local broadcast. Local station newscasts are usually the greatest single source of an affiliate's revenues.

At one time the network-news time slot was crucial in the battle for ratings, because it signaled the first prime-time network hookup of the evening. This resulted in intense kinetic competition among the networks to gain the largest newscast audience. Color cameras, videotape, interviews, and saturated "coverage" of events all served to embellish "the story." During the Nixon administration, there was growing pressure by the FCC to limit control of individual stations by the networks. This resulted in FCC legislation which released the half-hour following the network news back to the affiliate for purposes of increasing community identification with that station. In effect, the strength of the network news as a lead-in to prime-time was reduced, resulting in an eventual reduction in news budgeting.

On the other hand, competition at the eight o'clock time slot intensified. Once again the FCC intruded, deeming certain hours desirable for "family" viewing, with more "adult" programs to be slated later in the evening. One indirect result of this scheduling alignment was to actually reduce competition among the networks, for scheduling similar shows at the same time results in a narrowing of the type of programing available at any given hour. In order to get an overall view of TV programing, it became necessary to watch TV at all hours. Those who turned on the set at, say, ten o'clock in the evening were less likely to catch a half-hour situation comedy than those who tuned in earlier in the evening.

The horizontal and vertical schedule structures combine to form another structure, the weekly program schedule, which in turn serves the season schedule. The season schedule's purpose is to introduce new programs while eliminating failing ones. Shows that succeed and endure over several seasons enter into syndication, which is still another structure. When a show has exhausted its syndication play-off, it has completed the cycle— not because it has lost its entertainment value but because it has simply utilized all available formats.

Just as there is this external structure, there is also an internal structure, designed to maintain an audience through the run of a series, episode after episode, week after week, season after season, resulting in programs that (as in the case of situation comedies, for example) are funny, exciting, contemplative, verbal, and very much like all the others of that particular series, which are in turn very much like other successful series that preceded it. Successful scripts are those that appear fresh and new, yet don't break any new ground. The incessant laugh tracks continually urge the viewer to laugh along with the crowd, an act of intimidation suggesting that ''group laughter'' is a way of participating in the social mainstream. Not laughing becomes a passive, antisocial, even rebellious act.

The need for conformity is so great that the opportunity for creative breakthrough is severely limited. The reasons for this are twofold. First, the economic risk is too great to allow much experimentation; success on television being economic rather than artistic. A successful show is one that is watched by a lot of people, resulting in huge ad rates and revenues. Viewers understand this clearly. It comes as no surprise when a highly praised show such as "The Paper Chase" fails, while a show such as "Three's Company" succeeds. Ultimately, "Three's Company" is better show because it's more popular. Low ratings produce dwindling audiences. Watching a show that is "unpopular" is intimidating; underscored by the fact that more people are watching something else at the same time, something more successful.

III

MYTH: TELEVISION IS AN OUTGROWTH OF RADIO, THE
TECHNOLOGICAL ADDITION OF PICTURES TO
WORDS

FACT: The earliest experiments in television and radio technology occurred simultaneously during the first years of the twentieth century, well before either medium had become a major form of entertainment. Both began as communication devices, instruments for the transportation of messages from points of origin outside the studio. Neither was originally conceived as a source of entertainment. Television's creative history begins when programs are conceived for and broadcast from studios. Radio and television are similar in origin, but neither is derived from the other.

Widespread commercial network television would have been a reality by the early forties had America not entered into World War II. The war effort brought a temporary curtailment to the development and progress of commercial television broadcasting. Radio, however, already commercially established, flourished as a way of keeping people informed of events overseas; a form of reinforcement and reassurance for the electronic community, "uniting" them through a common voice.

Television's technological growth resumed after the war. By 1949 there were four networks broadcasting entertainment fare. (The fourth network, Dumont, went out of business in 1955 due to an inability to line up enough affiliate stations.) If radio then suffered, it was in the temporary loss of many of its stars to television, a process not widespread until well into the fifties, after the early success of Milton Berle, a performer who had not done that well in radio or the movies and therefore had less to lose experimenting in the new medium than did Jack Benny, George Burns, or Arthur Godfrey. If television's development hadn't been halted during the forties, radio's monopoly of talent wouldn't have existed. If anything, television's popular growth during the fifties hastened radio's reemergence in the sixties, after a severe economic slump, as the strong arm of the recording industry, complete with expanded FM band, fresh FCC regulations requiring programing on FM to be different from existing programing on AM, and an improved sound quality crucial to the marketing of records and, eventually, tapes. Today, radio is economically healthier than ever before. Its annual advertising revenues in the forties were calculated in the millions; today the figures run into the billions. Radio and television continue to progress, related but independent; sharing coverage of news and sports, maintaining separate entertainment criteria.

MYTH: THE DECLINE IN MOVIE ATTENDANCE DURING THE LATE FORTIES AND EARLY FIFTIES WAS DUE TO THE NEW POPULARITY OF TELEVISION, WHICH IN TURN HASTENED THE END OF THE HOLLYWOOD MOVIE STUDIO SYSTEM

FACT: Postwar Hollywood was its own victim, having read its press notices while failing to see the handwriting on the wall. Hollywood's decline became evident during the late forties and early fifties, but it actually began nearly a decade earlier.

Hollywood was called upon during the war years to help the government sell the American point of view. Major directors, actors and studios were enlisted to make and distribute propaganda films, such as Frank Capra's *Why We Fight* series. John

Wayne "war" movies came complete with enlistment desks in theater lobbies for all the would-be Sergeant Strykers to take that first big step toward heroism. By 1945, Hollywood was firmly entrenched in the war effort. Its films reflected its politics. *Mission to Moscow*, a 1945 Warner Brothers propaganda movie uniting U.S. and Soviet diplomats in an effort to hasten the end of the war, was made with the highest official approval, FDR's White House.

A year later the war ended and the postwar Hollywood film era began with William Wyler's 1946 Academy-Award-winning *The Best Years of Our Lives*, a film about the problems of the postwar adjustment period for returning veterans, an apt metaphor for the movie industry itself. The slant of the Wyler film was decidedly whimsical, Hollywood's wish to return to the way it was before the war. If Hollywood sought to return to the thirties' "golden age", the country, was heading straight for the fifties.

The uneasy alliance with the Soviets was gone by 1949, a year that also saw the "fall" of "free" China and the rise of the Communist specter over the burgeoning paranoid political American horizon, put into sharp focus by Senator Joseph McCarthy. The cold war turned hot, Korea became the new battlefield, and Hollywood continued to flounder. By the early fifties, the industry could be roughly divided into two factions. "Old" Hollywood was dominated by pioneering moguls who had literally created the film industry, first-generation legends now seeing "red" where once they'd seen gold. Their desire to return to the glory days of the Hollywood star system was easy to understand. And for good reason. The previous decade, the patriotic "war" years, were great box office. The studios were now determined to "advance" to the past. This put them at odds with "new" Hollywood. Marlon Brando's electrifying trilogy—*A Streetcar Named Desire*, *On the Waterfront*, and *The Wild One*—signaled the new attitude in movies, anticipating what was to become the dominant social posture of America's postwar generation, the "teenage" fifties and sixties.

The old guard was fading fast. Clark Gable of *The Hucksters* (1947—"GABLE'S BACK AND GARSON'S GOT HIM") was a far cry from Clark Gable of *Gone With the Wind*. Errol Flynn, Tyrone Power, Gary Cooper, James Stewart, John Wayne, Dick

Powell, Robert Taylor, Humphrey Bogart, James Cagney and others represented nothing so much as a Hollywood generation of leading men growing old. The very stars so crucial to the war effort of the forties were now having trouble getting "big" pictures. Many tried, like Bogart, to produce independent features, and were unsuccessful. Others turned to character and supporting roles. Still others sought to continue making 1940s-type movies. John Wayne was making propaganda movies well into the fifties, films like *Big Jim McClain*, the adventures of a red hunter in Washington, D.C.

Meanwhile the new stars were rising. Besides Brando, there was the nihilistic James Dean and the neurotic Montgomery Clift. Brando, Dean and Clift weren't products of the studio system, the backbone of "old" Hollywood. All three came out of New York's two training grounds: the Broadway stage and, ironically, live television. All three actors made films for Elia Kazan— Brando did *Streetcar, Waterfront* and *Viva Zapata;* Dean, *East of Eden;* Clift, *The River*. Kazan would always be at odds with "old" Hollywood. He would be called up before HUAC (The House Un-American Activities Committee) to testify about alleged Communist activities. Out of the HUAC hearings came the notorious blacklist. The Hollywood Ten, a group of Hollywood professionals well celebrated for their refusal to testify before the committee, grabbed front-page headlines. Hollywood itself seemed to be on trial, and the government was dusting off the hot seat.

Almost from the moment the Second World War ended, the government began hurling antitrust and monopoly charges at the studios. A Supreme Court ruling in 1949 allowed the majors to choose two of their three branches of operation to continue, with the forced surrendering of one. The studios up to this time controlled production, distribution and exhibition. Most studios chose to relinquish their exhibition arms, which resulted in a more intense competition between studios and independents for theaters in which to show their movies. The studio suppression of the independent film was finally starting to break down, signaling the real beginning of the end of the studio-dominated era of the Hollywood movie. Forced to compete for the attention of filmgoers, as well as with free television, the studios resorted to the gimmicry of 3-D and CinemaScope, vistavision and stereophonic sound, applying these techniques to big-budget epics, hoping to rejuvenate their industry rather than reshape it. The country was looking toward the future, toward Brando, Dean and Clift, while Hollywood was looking over its shoulder trying to catch up with the present.

Toward the end of the fifties, the movie industry began to breathe some fresh air. The rise of independent feature led to more location shooting, away from the Hollywood back lots. For a while the studios were largely dormant, still memories of another time, resurrected finally by television's migration west in the late fifties, a move backed by corporate investment in the burgeoning electronic age.

Today the studios are turning out product at near capacity, sharing space and talent between movies and television. Pictures gross more than ever, cost more to make, and are seen by more people than at any other time in Hollywood's history. The networks are major investors in Hollywood, buying broadcast rights to feature films before a single frame is shot. Far from "destroying" Hollywood, television saved what was in fact an aging and possibly dying industry, pushing movies toward more sophisticated themes not easily handled on television, investing heavily in the industry and the dream. Hollywood responded eagerly, making movies. And advertising them on television, of course.

MYTH: TELEVISION WAS RESPONSIBLE FOR THE DECLINE IN BROADWAY BOX OFFICE DURING THE FIFTIES AND SIXTIES

FACT: Television's roots are closer to the theater than to any other form of entertainment. Television began commercial broadcasting in New York, home of the Broadway stage. In the early days of live TV there was a chronic shortage of product; Broadway plays were broadcast directly from the stage while being performed before live audiences. This practice was soon replaced by televised "versions" of Broadway plays, less expensive than prohibitive "remote" broadcasts. These were then replaced by the original television drama, or "teleplay," written by TV's first crop of writers, headed by Paddy Chayefsky and Rod Serling.

At best, TV stylistics during the "golden age" of live broadcasting were exploratory and pragmatic. Upon subsequent viewing of shows it becomes clear that the "golden" quality of this period is better left to the vaults of memory, out of general circulation. The sheer primitiveness of the writing and performing, as well as the obvious technical crudeness, explain at least in part why few of the kinescopes, films, or videotapes of these productions have appeared on television in recent years.

These early TV shows were dramatic failures—experimental broadcasting rather than experimental drama. TV was a training ground, a place to fail. Consider a comparison between the most revered Broadway play of its day, Tennessee Williams' *The Glass Menagerie*, and the most often cited television play of the "golden age," Paddy Chayefsky's *Marty*.

Both plays deal with a young man's attempt to break away from the emotional and physical boundaries of youth, heredity and environment. In Williams' play the notion of breaking away is extended metaphorically to spiritual flights of youthful fancy, a poetic passion play graced with a special sense of distance—the distance of time, the gauzy link between memory and emotion. Chayefsky's teleplay is a neorealistic hunk of life—prosaic in its depiction of Marty's literal stumbling toward his destiny as a way out of his past. Williams' poetics are dramatized through the rhythmic distance of time, while Chayefsky's dramatics deal with the limitations of his physical space. Whereas Tom escapes his past through the distance of his lifetime, Marty simply moves out of his mother's apartment and down the block with the woman he's tripped over at the dance. Tom tries to sever his emotional dependency on the past when he leaves home. Marty substitutes one mother figure for another.

That Williams' play is superior is without question. What is important to note is that Chayefsky's play appears to be derived from the best Broadway play of the day, and suffers by comparison. Chayefsky, at the first blush of real success, would abandon TV writing in favor of the Broadway stage and eventually Hollywood. What was beneficial to TV about Chayefsky's and Serling's plays, along with the rest of the first-generation TV writers, was that while their work today seems dated and trivial, they were instrumental in gaining adult respect, along with significant ratings, for a medium then in the grip of "Howdy Doody." Yet, while exposure to TV drama may have encouraged some people to go see a Broadway play, it is far less likely that TV drama was compelling enough to keep theatergoers from seeing the major Broadway plays of the day. If anything, television may have helped to free the stage from its realistic fifties period, moving it toward a more commercial theater and the experimental Off-Broadway movement of the early sixties.

Once it migrated west, television shed itself of its need for "respectability." Tabloid adventures such as "Seventy-seven Sunset Strip" and "Maverick" proved enormously popular with viewing audiences, in spite of their lack of "relevance" and "dramatic profundity." To date, the history of American television is still analyzed, by and large, with reverence toward the "golden age" of live New York TV, and with, at best, tolerance toward the West Coast era of TV programing, where, of course, all the action really was.

IV

The fifties was a decade that saw furious attacks on the entertainment industry in America. Television brought much of the controversy home, in more ways than one.

By televising the McCarthy hearings during the early fifties, TV gave a public, national voice to a situation that may not otherwise have had the same dramatic impact. The televised McCarthy hearings gave TV an immediate boost as a relevant medium even as they threatened to inflict permanent damage on its industrial future. On the one hand, television produced Edward R. Murrow, the official "people's" voice against Senator McCarthy, while on the other hand it fervently employed a blacklist to keep out those tainted by the specter of Communism. Further, the televising of the Army/ McCarthy hearings became, in effect, television's first "series." It had repetition and continuity, a preoccupation with starting and ending on time, a "jury" (committee) as viewing audience, and stark images of heroes and villains played by "good" lawyer Joseph Welch and "bad" Senator Joseph McCarthy.

The government had already investigated the theater, effectively ending the Federal Theater, and was winding down its investigation of the movie industry. Now it was time to turn to television, perhaps to get a foothold in the new medium before things got too far out of hand. In 1961 the FCC was chaired by Newton F. Minow, who delivered the message quite clearly in his now celebrated "vast wasteland" speech, a phrase which became part of the American vernacular, an accusation that touched all of television, indicting not only the networks but the viewing audience as well. Minow rode moral shotgun over the airwave territory and threatened to mortally wound the industry's quest for respectability (and big bucks). Minow's blow was traumatic, the implication of moral waste opening the way for stiffer, unchallenged governmental regulations, allowing the FCC increased say as to what "should" and "should not" be broadcast. The most immediate and obvious results were a reduction in TV "violence"; "guidelines" were introduced as to what should be seen, when it should be seen, and, ultimately, if it should be seen.

V

Crime never pays. Criminals are never rehabilitated, penal institutions don't exist. Rehabilitation isn't necessary; removal from society is.

Husbands and wives don't engage in sex, they raise children. Pretty children are popular, ugly children cynical. Husbands die young or simply disappear. Mothers never work, single women always do. Housewives are slightly overweight, tired-looking and worry.

Money doesn't exist. The sixties never existed. The fifties began in the seventies. Heroes are handsome. Anything funny happens indoors. All problems are solved in slightly less than half an hour.

Nobody gets divorced. Nobody really dies. Nobody is really born. Sex, therefore, is unnecessary, therefore doesn't exist. Politics doesn't exist. America is in love with soft toilet paper, the taste of rich coffee, designer jeans and fast cars. Everyone has given up smoking. Nobody who's any good drinks. Beer is for pouring, but not for drinking.

Religion means church, church means Sunday, God isn't funny. All jokes are, though.

Automobiles screech when they come to a stop. Action is a fast-moving car.

Blacks are white, Puerto Ricans are black, Jews are Protestants. Irish peel anything, including soap; Italians lust after women; old people are little children; little children are adults. Marijuana is heroin; policemen in uniform don't like detectives; detectives are rich, have lots of hair and drive convertibles. All detectives live in Southern California. All uniformed cops are young.

The United States is a union of six states: New York, Los Angeles, Minneapolis-St. Paul, Chicago, Las Vegas, The Highway.

Women are tall, Bob Hope is the King of America, the President of the United States is the Bob Hope of politics. Walter Cronkite is the father of our country, rock and roll is legal after midnight, Johnny Carson and Ed McMahon drink and don't like women (they've each been married fifteen times, the divorces weren't their fault). Dick Cavett is smarter than Mike Douglas, who's too old anyway; Dinah Shore is thirty, used to love Burt Reynolds, and likes to cook a lot. Charlie's Angels are virgins, they work for Donovan's brain, and the government of the United States is involved in nothing and interferes with nobody.

TWO

The Shows

The following is a selective breakdown of the network prime-time scheduling formats of the past thirty years. The order of placement is chronological, except when a grouping of shows necessitates a break in the specific chronology. However, the general flow is from the late forties to the present. Shows have been included if they meet the following requirements:

1. They appeared for a full season on a prime-time network schedule (unless the complete run was for less than a season; or the show was cancelled).
2. They reflect certain stylistic, technical, or social aspects that illustrate the structure of television format, either internal or external.
3. Several episodes were actually viewed.

THE TEXACO STAR THEATER—THE MILTON BERLE SHOW: June 8, 1948–June 14, 1955, NBC.
Producer: Henry Jaffee Enterprises

Milton Berle's TV career in the fifties was scattered among various shows, the dates above more or less setting the formal beginning and end of his Tuesday-night reign of humor as NBC's "Mr. Television." Berle was one of the less glowing stars of forties radio, and not exactly a star in movies either. His resulting television success was therefore a surprise to everyone, himself included. Perhaps he was the first network variety star because he was willing to take the chance and go with the new medium. Unlike Benny or Hope, he didn't have that much to lose if he failed. Working with little more than an oh-gosh, oh-gee, I'm-so-happy-to-be-here enthusiasm, Berle substituted energy for entertainment, and volume for wit. He rightly surrounded himself with lots of talent to cover his own inability to entertain. Berle's dressing up in women's clothes grew out of a onetime skit that got a lot of laughs and was incorporated as part of his "act." His influence, then, is more iconographic than legendary; there are pioneers and there are pioneers. He was washed up by the end of the fifties, reduced to hosting an unsuccessful bowling show for NBC: If Berle makes us think of the fifties, the fifties don't make us think of Berle. And that's his failure, not ours.

THE ED SULLIVAN SHOW: June 20, 1948–June 6, 1971, CBS.
Producers: Ed Sullivan, Bob Precht

Ed Sullivan's impact was greatest before the development and widespread acceptance of videotape in the late fifties and early sixties. For many years after these technical advances were introduced, Sullivan refused to surrender his "live" format for tape, preferring the tension of going "on the air" to the safety and distance of being "prerecorded." Sullivan even refused to let singers lip-sync records, or dancers prerecord their lavish arrangements. He sensed, correctly, the need for the element of risk in going live. He was basically a journalist with a sense for the immediacy of the event, rather than the historical perspective of the performance. It was his journalistic present-tense preference that made watching him obligatory at eight o'clock on Sunday evenings.

Live from Manhattan, Sullivan would introduce celebrities seated in his audience, sometimes having them stand to take a bow, sometimes inviting them onstage to say a few words. Occasionally, as was the case with Fred Astaire, they would perform a number—seemingly spontaneously, actually a well-rehearsed plug for an upcoming show. What made this star-in-the-audience concept so effective was that Sullivan always seemed to be pointing at the camera when he was picking out the stars, as if the home audience were an extension of the studio audience, bringing the electronic audience closer to the action, not removing it further from it.

Sullivan's programing savvy still stands as the best; the timely, heroic athlete, Roberta Peters, Señor Wençes, Broadway casts performing scenes from current hits. Elvis Presley and the Beatles are unthinkable as culture phenomena apart from television, specifically their respective landmark appearances on Ed Sullivan. Presley's career had plodded along unimportantly until he began to appear on TV, and the controversial from the waist-up-only Presley camera work, dictated by Sullivan himself, was perhaps more responsible than anything else for the Presley craze, and all of what happened with rock and roll and the sixties that followed. Similarly, the Beatles weren't made in America on record until they were made on American TV. Without question Presley and the Beatles were TV stars first; record stars second. One could fetch farther than to suggest that Sullivan's rejection of Bob Dylan was one of the major reasons that Dylan was never as commercially successful as either Presley or the Beatles.

And of course there were the controversies unique to live TV: the feud with Jack Paar over how much to pay guests, and how soon they could appear on Paar's NBC nightly program after having been on his (Sullivan's) show; the blacklisting of Larry Adler and Paul Draper; the last-minute canceling of the Bob Dylan appearance because of a dispute over lyrics; the banishment of Jackie Mason for allegedly giving Sullivan the finger on network TV; the furious ratings battle with Steve Allen that erupted into personal mudslinging.

Yet, for all the tough tabloid one-twos Sullivan used off-camera, his TV persona was of the grand, yet humble stoic: "Old Stone Face." Nothing seemed to please him more than to have comedians come on the show to impersonate him. This was a shrewd move, for, besides telling the world he could laugh at himself, it also reinforced, quite effectively, his legend as much as his image. And Sullivan knew how to sell the legend while remaining very much his own man, a quite professional and flexible human being with an ego the size of his stage and a sense of bravura as great as Flo Ziegfeld's.

TED MACK'S ORIGINAL AMATEUR HOUR: January 18, 1949–September 1971, Dumont/ABC/NBC/CBS.
Producer: Ted Mack

ARTHUR GODFREY'S TALENT SCOUTS: December 6, 1948–July 21, 1958, CBS.
Producers: Irving Mansfield, Jack Carney

Both of these shows presented "talent" in a medium itself still experimental in the late forties, when the gap between "amateur" and "professional" wasn't yet all that great. As television rapidly developed, the notion of the amateur on screen became more pejorative. Today's descendant of both Ted Mack and Arthur Godfrey is Chuck Barris.

That Godfrey's arrogance in dealing with his presentation of "talent" was up front, while Ted Mack's was more subtle, being swathed in pity, ultimately makes little difference, for neither host ever let us forget just who was in the pilot's seat. Godfrey sat high above where the "talent" performed, his posture and delegatory gestures making him seem even more important, more professional, in contrast to the stumbling, nervous newcomers he was blessing with his presence. If the "Amateur Hour" played upon the cliché that you could begin the day an unknown and end it a star, Godfrey's show made you question why you'd want to be a star in the first place.

HOPALONG CASSIDY: June 24, 1949–December 23, 1951, NBC.
Producers: William Boyd, Toby Anguist
99 episodes

THE LONE RANGER: September 15, 1949–September 12, 1957, ABC.
Producers: Sherman Harris, George W. Trendle, Jack Chertok, Harry Pope
221 episodes

THE GENE AUTRY SHOW: July 23, 1950–August 7, 1956, CBS.
Producers: Armand Schaefer for Flying A Productions
85 episodes

THE ROY ROGERS SHOW: December 30, 1951–June 23, 1957, NBC.
Producers: Jack Lacey, Bob Henry, Roy Rogers, Leslie H. Martinson
100 episodes

The first TV cowboys kept the children entertained. If no one seemed to care very much what they were up to, the stars of these shows were no fools. One by one they made their fortunes in the burgeoning TV market—Roy Rogers, Gene Autry, and William Boyd (Hopalong Cassidy) each made millions through shrewd negotiations for the TV rights to their theatrical movies.

As for the shows themselves, they varied slightly from one to the next. Essentially there were the good guys and the bad guys, the endlessly firing six-shooters, the bruiseless fights, the obligatory companions. Roy Rogers had Pat Brady (and Dale), Gene Autry had Pat Buttram, Hoppy had Red Conners (Edgar Buchanan), and of course the Lone Ranger (Clayton Moore) had

Tonto (Jay Silverheels). The sidekicks served dual purposes. First, they were always more grotesque-looking than the heroes, accentuating the mythic good looks of the heroic good guy. Second, with the exception of Dale Evans, they kept the women away, important for horse-over-lady pre-teen priorities.

At any rate, the tension of "Gunsmoke" wouldn't have been possible without the tinsel of Hoppy. To deny television its growing pains is to deny television its eventual maturity.

THE LIFE OF RILEY: October 4, 1949–August 22, 1958, NBC.
Producer: Irving Brecher, Tom McKnight
117 episodes (26 original version, 91 second version)

The first run of this series, late in the forties, produced by Irving Brecher, starred Jackie Gleason in the title role. The more successful version, produced by Tom McKnight, replaced Gleason with William Bendix, and it was then that the series really took off.

Chester A. Riley (Bendix) was the epitome of the post-World War II husband and father—a man now at war with the institution of marriage, willing to surrender his life in defense of his wife's right to harass him. Married to "field marshal" Peg (Marjorie Reynolds), whose most memorable quality was looking slightly to the right of Riley when she spoke to him, his only refuge and friend was Gillis (Tom D'Andrea), who understood Riley, being on the same front lines battling his own wife, Honeybee (Gloria Blondell).

This program was extremely popular in its Friday night prime-time network slot. What better time for the Rileys all across America to settle down in their favorite easy chair after a hard week at the plant, open up a can of beer and commiserate electronically with their TV counterpart while the kids kicked up a storm and the wife complained about needing a new washing machine? Small comfort to know that the armchair suffering was not being done in isolation—a special entree to self-delusion, believing one was living the life of Riley while watching it.

**YOUR SHOW OF SHOWS: February 25, 1950–June 5, 1954,
                        NBC.
Executive Producer: Max Liebman**

**SATURDAY NIGHT LIVE: October 11, 1975–still
                        running, NBC.
Executive Producer: Lorne Michaels**

The first thing that comes to mind about "Your Show of Shows" is Sid Caesar's cough. It was one of those little things that made Caesar memorable. His show, rather than shying away from the vulnerabilities of "going live," as the turgid "golden age of TV drama" did, played upon them, having the effect of bringing us closer rather than keeping us away.

The combined writing and acting talents of Caesar, Carl Reiner, Howard Morris and Imogene Coca (later replaced by Gisele MacKenzie) delivered, week after week, the finest entertainment on television. Caesar's best satires were of domestic life and the movies. Anyone who's seen his parody take-offs of Marlon Brando in *On the Waterfront*, or of Burt Lancaster in *From Here to Eternity*, or his reluctant subject of "This is your Life" was privileged to an incredible demonstration of wit, physical comedy, and intellectual nuance. By going after Brando's brawn rather than his mumble, Caesar was able to focus on Brando's sensuality rather than his brutishness, as opposed to the hundreds of second-rate "Stellah"-shouting Brando impersonators of the day. Caesar at once not only made the definitive satiric comment on Brando, but also on method acting and its link to American movies in the fifties.

"Saturday Night Live" brings live TV variety full circle. Its ensemble cast is no less effective than Caesar's, sometimes better, willing to go further out on a limb. Whereas Caesar's humor was equally effective when dealing with suburbia, the movies, or television, the "Saturday Night" crew is, at best, uneven. When they are good they're great, when they are bad they're awful. Their only legitimate realm of satire was television itself. The show's original cast—John Belushi, Chevy Chase, Dan Ackroyd,

Gilda Radner, Jane Curtin, Bill Murray, Garrett Morris, and Laraine Newman—represented the first generation of TV kids who grew up on Pablum, formula and "Howdy Doody." Their satire reached all the way back to Gleason's "Honeymooners" and all the way forward to political merchandising. Ackroyd's Julia Child, Belushi's Gleason, Chase's Jerry Ford, Radner's Rosanne Rosaannadanna, Murray's Ted Kennedy, and Morris' Anwar Sadat were superb TV satire, the accent always on the political image in the media rather than issues and politics. As for the newer "players," it's too soon as of this writing for any serious evaluation.

The show's take-offs of TV commercials remind us how easily the public is sold a product (or a politician) if packaged attractively. The Gubners remind us that we don't really care about the characters in situation comedies, but rather the performers who play them. If there is reverence for anything on "Saturday Night Live" it's for the TV generation's own music, rock and roll, which is why Ricki Lee Jones, Billy Joel, Mick Jagger, Paul Simon, Bob Dylan, George Harrison, and the B-52's will appear on the show. On rare occasions, when rock and roll was the target rather than the shrine, as with Belushi and Ackroyd's Blues Brothers, the audience was so used to reverence that what started out as a gag became a best-selling album and a thirty-million-dollar movie.

THE JACK BENNY PROGRAM: October 28, 1950–September
                    10, 1965, CBS/NBC.
Producers: **Hilliard Marks, Seymour Berns, Ralph Levy, Fred**
                 Decordova, Irving Fein
343 episodes

If Ed Sullivan's was the image of the awkward American, Jack Benny's was the epitome of the paranoid refugee. Working off the grim cliché of the "cheap Jew," he was able to mock both the cliché and those who bought it.

Benny was paterfamilias of a wonderful family of characters: Mary Livingston, Dennis Day, Rochester, Mel Blanc, Don Wilson, Joe Besser, Barbara Nichols, among others. Watching Jack

Benny on TV was to see him at "home" with his friends and relatives, within an electronic European-style communal "home base" as central locus for the action.

Benny, who had been on the radio for many years, made the switch to TV better than anyone else because, unlike those who merely continued their radio and movie persona from one medium to the other, Benny was able to correct his skills from the aural to the video. Example: On the radio his most famous gag was the pause. While being held up and threatened with "Your money or your life," the long silence that followed became, in fact, the punch line. On TV the pause turned into the stare, complete with palm on face, and the transformation was complete.

Jack Benny seemed to mock and shun the medium of television itself, preferring to remain "one of the people." His shows were always flashbacks of one time or another, to that afternoon's rehearsal, or to an evening earlier in the week at a restaurant, perhaps in Beverly Hills like the one where he was having dinner when James Stewart happened to be there. Jack, thinking Stewart was his best friend, pondered whether he should go over and say hello or not, while Stewart squirmed and fretted over how to avoid the annoying comedian.

Or the time he was "dating" (Mary Livingston, his wife in real life, was only his "girlfriend" on the show, as Benny sought to avoid the husband-wife cliché, fearing it would narrow his range of comedy) and took his girlfriend to a small, crowded restaurant. The only table available was a tiny one in the corner. At first refusing to take it, his mind was easily changed once he realized they wouldn't be able to order as much food since there was very little room to put it on. Or the evening he was held up and robbed, then forced to open his vault for the robbers, which involved a hilarious journey through the depths of his "mansion," playing once again on the myth of the miser, bringing the illogical to the surface by taking the myth to the limit. Or the violin contest he had with Gisele MacKenzie, when it seemed that they were trying to prove who was the worst while trying to show who was the best. Or, or, or. . . .

Jack Benny's place in the *oeuvre* of American humor is unique. He was clever without conceit, authoritative without being abrasive, graceful without being weak. His humor was filled with an

Old World wisdom—sophisticated, complex, yet plainly funny. He was television's Thornton Wilder, classically articulate in the common idiom.

BROADWAY OPEN HOUSE—THE TONIGHT SHOW—TONIGHT—AMERICA AFTER DARK—THE JACK PAAR SHOW—THE TONIGHT SHOW—THE TONIGHT SHOW STARRING JOHNNY CARSON: May 29, 1951–still running, NBC.
Various producers.   Present producer: Fred Decordova

Hosting "The Tonight Show" is a difficult assignment. He, or she, must be pleasant, and if possible, less a distraction than an attraction, so that the focus may be shared between host and guest. "The Tonight Show" set is a desk and chair, more like an office than a stage, the chatter more like an interview than a conversation. Many years ago Jerry Lewis tried to introduce a more visual aspect to a similar network talk show by having his stage, for no known reason, go up and down like an elevator. His show lasted six weeks before being replaced with one that had a stationary stage.

Over the years NBC's late-night "Tonight Show" has actually been a series of individual talk shows linked together by time slot and format: live band, live audience, live host, live announcer, mostly live guests. The view from here:

Jerry Lester's "Broadway Open House" was boring, leering, unintelligent, too much deli, not enough soufflé. Dagmar didn't help, but this was TV's infancy, when the notion of being on television was itself enough of a curiosity factor to warrant tuning in. Lester and Co. proved nothing beyond the fact that they had no idea how to fill the time.

Steve Allen, on the other hand, was excellent in the host seat, perhaps the true originator of the talk-show format. He implemented desk-and-chair give-and-take, being intelligent, offbeat, musical, courageous, original, if perhaps a bit overly dependent on audience participation; and all that orange juice was a bit too

West Coast for its time. Nevertheless he created the New York TV ambiance of late-night entertainment. He called upon a regular set of young, unknown cabaret singers to gig in rotation, giving career boosts to the likes of Steve Lawrence, Eydie Gormé, Andy Williams, and others. Ahead of the network's time, he was never again able to achieve the power or status he had while at the helm of "Tonight."

Jack Paar was the best of the "Tonight Show" hosts. He elicited extreme reactions, pro and con, always holding his audience riveted. His string of guests were the most interesting, informed, opinionated and articulate on the air: Alexander King, Genevieve, Jack Douglas, Oscar Levant; TV's version of the Algonquin roundtable. Paar didn't give a damn about plugs, pre-interviewing, or sponsors. His stuttering made him real, and Hugh Downs's sophistication make Paar seem more of an ordinary guy than he really was. José Melis (on piano) added a bit of international flavoring to the show. Paar's celebrated walk-out while on the air sent shockwaves through the network and proved just how powerful and popular Paar was. The network wouldn't forget this power play, and when Paar eventually left "The Tonight Show" for good, NBC buried him in a weekly time slot where he could show home movies, to no one's great annoyance or concern. Few people realize today that it was Paar, not Sullivan, who first gave America the Beatles, which says a lot about their respective showmanship. "The Tonight Show" switched from live to tape during Paar's tenure, a factor that, more than anything else, led to his giving up the show; for if any performer in live television demanded the present-tension, it was Paar.

Johnny Carson was next in line to fill the slot, and it is to his credit that he took over and made the show his own. After promising at the start not to make waves, Carson went on to become the most political commentator on television, surpassing the editorial aspects of the network news, surpassing even Bob Hope in the role of official court jester while always making sure, as Hope did, that the boat never rocked too much, that governmental criticism was kept squarely in the official posture of humor, rather than in the pointed stance of accusation. As a result, Carson's politics blurred—sometimes to the right, as when attacking government spending or Governor Jerry Brown; sometimes to the left, when mocking President Reagan and Jimmy Carter.

Johnny's best moments come after his monologue and before the first guest, when, along with the chronically hysterical Ed McMahon, he indulges in routines that have the look of classic comedy, if in fact they aren't the greatest moments in humor. Johnny: "I have here everything you ever wanted to know about peanut butter . . ." McMahon, astonished: "You mean to sit there and tell us that you have everything . . . EVERY-THING . . ." Or Carnac: "This is the final envelope . . ." followed by an ovation from the audience. Or the used-car salesman. He does them all, if not all that well, perhaps his secret for being around so long.

THE RED SKELTON SHOW: September 30, 1951–August 29, 1971, NBC/CBS.
Producers: Gerald Gardner, Dee Caruso

"Beloved" is a word that should be reserved for the departed. Its show-business meaning, in particular, is coded—meaning too old to work but not yet dead. Red Skelton is a case in point. His TV career declined in direct proportion to his belovedness. The fact is, he was the only legitimate clown television ever had.

Red Skelton was CBS's successful answer to NBC's Milton Berle. Berle held forth on Tuesday nights for five years; Skelton did it for twenty. He attained beloved status when CBS swept away the cobwebs at the end of the sixties, getting rid of Jack Benny, Ed Sullivan, and Skelton. While these performers were still getting sufficient numbers in the ratings, their numbers were getting old, with diminished purchasing power. Bits with sass were to be replaced by tits and ass.

Skelton's clowning was expressed through his numerous characterizations, including Freddie the Freeloader, Clem Cadiddlehopper, Sheriff Deadeye, Cauliflower McPugg, George Appleby, San Fernando Red. Freddie, in particular, was very much like Gleason's poor soul, Skelton having the edge on bitterness; Gleason opting for pity. All Skelton's characters were remarkably unsympathetic, the clown preferring to dwell on the cynical attitude of failure and the specter of old age. Skelton was alone among all TV performers in perceptively attuning his sensibilities to the senior citizen without the obligatory Valium-da-dum of Lawrence Welk, or the hyperactivity of Mrs. Odetts ("My Little Margie"). His refusal to contemporize his show with rock acts and young starlets spelled finis to his long run. It was however a TV death with dignity proof that the structure on television runs deep—demographics by pocketbook.

I LOVE LUCY: October 15, 1951–June 24, 1957, CBS.
Executive Producer: Desi Arnaz
179 episodes

"I Love Lucy" is the most popular American television program of all time, top-rated four of its six network years, second one year, third the other. In syndication since it left the network, the show is seen every day all over the world in every major television market, including Asia and Africa.

Based on the forties radio series "My Favorite Husband," which also starred Lucille Ball, "I Love Lucy" remains the prototypical situation comedy: half-hour, single-set construction (living room), a group of neighbors who appear regularly, a live audience on the sound/laugh track, heard but never seen. Audiences were invited to the filming of the episodes by Desi Arnaz, the shrewd producing arm of Desilu. It was Arnaz who introduced live audience and recorded laughs to television situation comedy, a move designed to bring out the best possible performance by Lucille Ball, whose talents Arnaz correctly figured would be better served by having her play to live audiences rather than on a closed sound stage where it would be difficult, if not impossible, to set the timing for all the physical gags the show used.

Lucy's living room was, by extension, Lucy's world. It offered limited lateral freedom while denying any upward mobility. Lucy's desire to be part of Ricky's (Desi Arnaz's) nightclub "act" was the pretext for many of the show's episodes. This desire to break out of the pleasant prison of her surroundings to perform in the nightclub of Desi's world was interpreted harmlessly in the preliberationist fifties, which viewed Lucy as brightly wacky rather than darkly absurdist; lovable housewife rather than frustrated woman.

Ricky, that crazy bumbling lovable Latin, would come to breakfast early in the morning in shirt and tie, read the papers over coffee, kiss his wife goodbye, and head off to his nine-to-five job as a nightclub performer. It was necessary to portray Ricky as the standard, respectable American hard-working husband, if for no other reason than to offset his "crazy Latin" image, a problem, unavoidable as much as it was unbelievable for Ricky to be a banker, a big-business executive, or a Latin lover. The solution was the compromise: part nightclub performer, part buffoon, part outsider, part respectable day-shift family man.

The landscape was further fleshed out by the presence of the Mertzes (William Frawley and Vivian Vance), ostensibly neighbors and landlords, in reality mother and father figures there to keep an eye on "the kids." Spats between the Ricardos were resolved more often than not by the paternal Mertzes. When Lucy and Ethel fought, the mother-daughter split was fused by the father-son axis. These mother-daughter feuds were nearly always bouts for authority, in which Lucy did something without Ethel's permission or awareness. This was further complicated when it involved Ricky's nightclub act, which Lucy, Ethel and Fred were always trying to join, proving either that they were all as talented as Ricky, or that Ricky had as little talent as they did.

Money was never a problem. The Ricardos were, at various times, middle-class, upper-class, and rich. Their upward mobility was proof that hard work and fidelity insured success, which made Lucy's desire to join Ricky onstage acceptable in non-liberationist terms. A good wife should help out at the store occasionally. In fact, this was a more easily acceptable idea than a good wife helping out in bed, occasionally or otherwise—hence a duo onstage okay, but twin beds at home. Lucy's desire to be "part of the act" led to the solution that kept her at home once and for all. The arrival of "Little Ricky" gave Lucy what-for for wanting to bang Ricky's congos. Having a baby solved the "problem" of what to do with her life, if it didn't exactly explain what Lucy's problem was in the first place any more than it clarified the confused metaphor of Lucy onstage for Lucy in bed. The very revelation of being pregnant was a major problem for the show and for the CBS network, which saw the saving grace in Lucille Ball's real-life pregnancy as the only way to explain Lucy's condition—the word "pregnant" still a no-no on television, let alone the visual presence of a woman "with child." If the night-club career of Ricky Ricardo was necessarily stylized in order to clean up his act, Lucy's pregnancy was absolutely sterilized. The first TV "birth" also produced the first stylized "death"—the gradual relegation of the parental reign of the Mertzes; a shift in emphasis to the new arrival. This upsetting of the sitcom balance signaled the peak of the show's success and the start of its comic decline.

Lucille Ball's Lucy was the model for the long string of sitcom femmes that followed, as was Ricky's ba-ba-loo-brained husband for the passive, fear-of-female house husband. The show set formulaic guidelines that are still very much in use today. Laugh tracks are still getting hysterical over these Lucy-inspired rules of the game: Lie to your husband if you think you can get away with it, as long as you understand in the end you'll never get away with it, but you'll be forgiven anyway. Be honest if it's convenient, but remember honesty is dull and, even worse, unfunny; desception, hilarious but unworkable. Forgiveness is obligatory, understanding the sign of true love and eternal wisdom.

Lucy's predicaments and resolutions set the sitcom standard on TV for nearly twenty years, until Norman Lear shook it all up by putting a toilet in the Archie Bunker household, allowing America to deal with a complex protagonist with more than a conga drum between his legs.

I MARRIED JOAN: October 15, 1952–April 6, 1955, NBC.
Producers: Dick Mack, J. Wolfson
98 episodes

On the heels of the success of CBS's "I Love Lucy" came NBC's "I Married Joan." If Lucy proved to be the more popular series, it was because Joan (Joan Davis) displayed a quality totally lacking in Lucy: humility. This gave Joan an edge that made the show less funny, less slapstick, yet more sublime, certainly more subtle. The pneumatic drilling of Lucy's boyish humor proved, after all, to be more to the public's liking than the soft probing of Joan's feminine pick.

Joan's husband, Domestic Relations Court Judge Bradley Stevens (Jim Backus), was seen at the start of each episode high on his bench, handing down a decision. To illustrate why he'd ruled the way he had, he would recount an episode in his own life, forming the basis of that week's half-hour. The viewpoint here was always the husband's (with "Lucy" it was always the wife's). This enabled us to see Joan's vulnerable side without accompanying self-pity. If Lucy was able to dominate Ricky with the grace of selfless physical energy, Joan's attempts at handling the judge were merely self-conscious and clumsy. She was a homely klutz in a world of official and emotional authority where her only reward was not being punished. Joan's redemption came from the audience, guided along by the sweetly stylistic chorus of chanting voices used to verbally dissolve scenes, and Joan's endless plights, replacing preliberationist struggle with whimsical fairy-tale flight. In the end, the titles told the tales. Ricky may have loved Lucy, but the judge married Joan.

**AMOS AND ANDY: June 28, 1951–June 11, 1953, CBS.
Producers: James Fonda, Freeman Gosden, Charles Correll
78 episodes**

"Amos and Andy" is the finest situation comedy series ever produced. Unfortunately, the show was a victim of paranoid times and subjected to the social sanitizing that began in the fifties and continued well into the sixties, all but washing the ethnic spirit of America out of the hair of the mass media.

Such '50s shows as "I Remember Mama," "The Goldbergs," and "Amos and Andy" "overcame" the "problem" of ethnicity by virtue of attitude, finding consequence and drama in the exploration of various class and racial problems on an individual basis. The success of a 1970s "black" show such as "The Jeffersons" rests in its across-the-races reflection of mass social advance, the result of suppressed individuality.

The "Amos and Andy" show had several generations of success on the radio before coming to television. The two main characters, Amos (Freeman Gosden) and Andy (Charles Correll), black characters portrayed by white men, were examples of "aw shucks" wisdom from the Will Rogers school of humor. When the show shifted to television its two creators drew the line at donning blackface, producing instead the first all-black television network program; a series with wit, insight, superior acting, and a level of situation comedy previously (and since) unseen.

Tim Moore's George Kingfish Stevens defined once and forever the American henpecked husband dominated by his beautiful, intelligent wife, in this case Sapphire (Ernestine Wade). While living in fear of his overpowering mother-in-law (Amanda Randolph), the Kingfish found male refuge in the private sanctum of "The Lodge"—The Mystic Knights of the Sea— with his best friend Andy, Andrew J. Brown (Spencer Williams, Jr.). Having seen it, who can ever forget the Kingfish walking down the steps of his Harlem brownstone tenement, thrown out of his house by the one-two punch of wife and mother-in-law, carrying all his meaningful possessions with him: suitcase, fedora, and that painting he insisted was his?

Andy, the Kingfish's bosom buddy, was that eternal adolescent pal who, like his friend, found the state of marriage completely unfathomable, and, unlike his friend, realistically unnecessary. Sex seemed out of the question, anyway. The twist here was that Sapphire wasn't a monster at all, rather a loving, beautiful and intelligent wife with feelings and empathy for her husband. Her weakness was also George's, if not in exactly the same way. Her mother was her protector, defending her from her husband, keeping him from her daughter. The influence of mother over husband placed Sapphire squarely on the adolescent stage. What we had here was a show not so much about adult marriage, sex, and repression as a show about the problem of transition from adolescence to adulthood, from both male and female points of view, leaving the nest in search of a nest egg.

Set in the solidly middle class Harlem of the late forties—early fifties, the show was an immediate success with a seemingly endless run ahead of it, until the paranoia of the McCarthy years and those that followed saw suspicion take precedence over investigation and supposition become more heroic than substantiation. Rather than being seen as a fabulous journey into the predisintegrating inner city of New York's black community, "Amos and Andy" was formally condemned by well-intentioned but misinformed black and white organizations. Rather than being racist, the show saw the beauty beneath the urban grime, and joy on the raised faces of its street-slick, if financially grim, compatriots in whimsical, adolescent rites of passage.

"Amos and Andy" didn't trade one-liners (as much as the original radio series did), preferring to find its humor in situations, and sophisticated ones at that. Like the time the Kingfish hauled his mother-in-law into domestic court, charging her with "interference" in his marriage. The judge, a white man, sat high on the bench and listened to both sides before ordering Mama to remain hereafter silent while in the Stevens household. Sapphire and Mama were temporarily defeated, but not yet ready to concede the war. They devised a scheme to teach George a lesson. They hired a friend to play George's "long lost" relative, just arrived in town and in need of a place to stay. Kingfish was grateful when Sapphire agreed to let George's "relation" stay. Soon, though, George's good feelings soured, as his "relative" proceeded to efficiently eat him out of house and home, to smoke him out of cigars and sanity. After failing in his own attempt to get his "relation" to leave, George finally turned to Sapphire for help. Sapphire agreed, but only after George promised that Mama could stay, without court regulations, for as long as she liked.

The brilliant turn here was that George never found out he'd been deceived. This worked because it relied on the basic good nature of the Kingfish for the logical basis of his behavior. It was Sapphire's trickery, a skill inherited from her mother, which played on George's generous instincts to trap him. We, along with George, were duped, for we weren't sure until the very end whether George's relative was legitimate or not. Nowhere was the standard TV cliché of having George "discover" the plot and then play along "for the fun of it," or of his teaching Sapphire and

Mama "a lesson" while they were in fact teaching him one. Also missing was the inevitable character change, TV's shortcut to dramatic denouement. This gimmick would have had George realizing he'd being duped by Sapphire and his mother-in-law, but, so what, lots of hugging, and letting Mama stay anyway.

A word about that white judge, so high on his bench, looking down on the people, an image not easily forgotten. Perhaps the NAACP should have fought to keep "Amos and Andy" on the air, if only to remind us of the matter-of-fact acceptance of such electrifying instances of racial outrageousness that were so much a part of the schemata of pre-sixties movies, theater, and television. Instead, the NAACP and other groups fought successfully to have the show banned from the airwaves. In 1966 "Amos and Andy," still in syndication re-run was removed from American television, if not from the American conscience, forever.

**ART LINKLETTER'S HOUSE PARTY: September 1,
          1952–September 5, 1969, CBS.**
Producer: Art Linkletter

PEOPLE ARE FUNNY: September 19, 1954–April 2, 1961, NBC.
Producer: Art Linkletter

Art Linkletter's TV career anticipated Phil Donahue's smiling-salesman appeal to the housewife. Linkletter's preliberationist "I understand, ladies" demeanor was his only angle, and he used it well, displaying a contrived back-porchism aimed at his housewife audience. And of course, when all else failed, there were always the children to play off, a surefire direct line to Mom.

Linkletter vanished from the networks when the sixties took over, only to return in the seventies still smiling, now pushing insurance to old folks by virtue of his virtue. Linkletter was, and is, a TV huckster, an electronic medicine man whose presence in the early days of TV did nothing to advance the medium, and probably helped to retard it. People are funny; hosts who laugh at them rather than with them aren't.

DRAGNET: December 16, 1951–September 10, 1970, NBC.
Executive Producer: Jack Webb
98 episodes

THE FUGITIVE: September 17, 1963–August 29, 1967, ABC.
Executive Producer: Quinn Martin
Producer: Wilton Schiller
120 episodes

"Dragnet" was the most perfect television series, if not the best. Jack Webb was instrumental in defining the stylistic possibilities of dramatic TV series fare, helping to wrench the medium out of its purely derivative theatrical mode, creating a context referring to itself purely in TV terms. The Webb techniques all but completed the stylistic innovation of the tube, after which a stylistic stasis would set in, encouraging little creative growth, producing technical refinement instead. However, by his use of cinema montage and close-up stylistics adapted for the small TV screen, Webb created a style very high and very dry, appropriate for his ominous, brilliant persona: the maniacal Sergeant Joe Friday.

There were no moral ambiguities in the world of "Dragnet." Pure authority reigned supreme. Sergeant Joe Friday's authority was fueled by his moral outrage, and from this outrage came his legal strength. The lack of moral ambiquity was reflected stylistically through a lack of visual ambiguity, hence the "Dragnet montage"—look here, look here, look here; the eye directed through the sequence of shots, usually close-ups of faces. This cut-cut-cut rhythm served to evoke the pulse of crime as well as that of the crime fighter, a stylistic blending of good and evil creating a tension the likes of which had never been seen before on television. Webb's fascination with the face of evil—the eyes, ears, nose and mouth of crime—reflected his repulsion with the elements of the enemy. When a criminal was to be sympathetically rendered (not morally deficient), such as the senile old lady who didn't "know" she was shoplifting, Webb would stylistically "keep his distance," using medium and full shots, leaving the woman within the context of her world, her image slightly reduced to describe her dwarfed sensibilities. When a criminal such as a killer, conman, or junkie, was morally guilty, though, the camera became relentless, the face of evil a mug shot, the surrounding world eradicated. Brought to justice, these criminals were left standing, after the last commercial, in moral limbo, less a courtroom than the gateway to hell. The final, real, terrifying punishment in "Dragnet" was banishment, without concern for rehabilitation, underscored by the voice of authority telling the world that the criminal was "*now* serving a fifteen-year sentence . . ."

The dialogue on "Dragnet" was direct, lacking adjectival color, because the camera did the real talking—or screaming, as it were. Sergeant Friday was almost always defined in medium, or medium close-up, his villains always in tight close-ups, creating a visual sense of conflict: St. George vs. the dragon. Friday's heroics were tempered by his contextual *mise-en-scene*. It was important to identify Friday as the common (law-abiding) man, through the small-talk chats with his partners about what they were going to do that weekend, drinking coffee out of containers, discussing the ball game the night before. Yet, wearing the common cloak, Friday clearly walked supreme. His heroics approached the divine, emphasized rather than reduced by his sparse surroundings: the simple desk in the simple police station, the stark interrogation room, the victim's house. Friday's was a world built on physical necessity, a state of morally civilized grace, contrasted with the moral emptiness, physical excess of the bloated face of crime.

"Dragnet" was a recurring nightmare week after relentless week. Its stylistics exploded the previously held notions about what could be done within the confines of twenty-one inches. A close-up of a man's face on TV is approximately the size of a man's face in real life, while in the movies a close-up explodes onto the giant screen creating a larger-than-life hero or villain. The difference between the stylistic tension of the movies and that of television is that the movies redeem by expanding the vision of dreams, bringing viewers a span that is larger than life. Simple acts become heroic in stature, if not in action, serving to enhance the notion of the heroic rebel. The romanticism of the movies expands the notion of Everyman as hero. Television, on the other hand, intrudes upon the everyday; reflecting, often reducing in the process the scope of the viewer, in a sense reinforcing the status quo rather than suggesting the option of rebellion. Television redefines the nature of the hero, suggesting that heroic stature maintains the status quo rather than rebels against it. The artistic challenge in working in television remains the exploration of intimacy rather than the packaging of images in miniature.

Finally, in "Dragnet," law and order operate in tandem with crime and anarchy. Since crime is ever present, the battle is better suited to the ongoing TV series form than, perhaps, the definitive two-hour feature film. Along with this, the challenge to the series is to find revelation within the endless continuum, to discover vital form within rigid format. "Dragnet" was first shot in black and white, another apt stylistic metaphor for the rigid Webb point of view. Eventually the show went to color, using the stark and overly contrasted TV tint to illustrate the garishness of the criminal world. Throughout the sixties Webb's desperate attempt to corral evil was slowly replaced by the aging Sergeant Friday's search for his own relevance in a world gone to drugs, hippies, rock and roll and anti-Americanism. Ever increasingly the plots of the shows turned toward the young as predator and the cop as victim. Friday's authority turned toward the religious as the dialogue became increasingly more preachy than pragmatic; the need to punish, a function of ageist philosophy as Friday grew older in a world growing younger. By 1967 "Dragnet" had become a Passion Play.

"Dragnet" was the most perfect TV series, but not the best. That was "The Fugitive," the intriguing dialectical complement to "Dragnet," filled with ambiguity and the universal pervasiveness of guilt. Richard Kimble (David Janssen), a doctor wrongly accused of murdering his wife, found a new sense of liberation through his official designation as criminal. The ironic twist of fate came while Kimble was on the way to the death house to face execution when a freak train accident "freed" him. This new "freedom" brought new burdens beyond the obvious and the expected. For one thing, it placed Kimble in the peculiarly ambivalent circumstance of having to fight for personal survival without being able to make any useful social contribution.

Robbed of his medical credentials, he was free to play out his wild, romantic flight of fancy. Kimble was the ultimate romantic, the metaphorical rebel in society perceiving social responsibility as creative imprisonment, social rejection as artistic liberation. His final victory, the capture and death of the one-armed man, was bittersweet, for while freeing him from his role of fugitive, it also restored him to his functionary chores as social healer. When Kimble looked over his shoulder for the last time in the final moments of the last episode, his first instinct was to run, to revert to his symbolic flight of fancy. He didn't flee because he couldn't. There was simply nowhere to go, and nothing to run from.

"The Fugitive" suggested that being on the run was a romantic notion filled with unknown adventure, exotic travel, unlimited sexual exploration. In effect, this view was existential, through the eye of the criminal; a deft twist, for while society considered Kimble a murderer (the antithesis of Dr. Kimble, saver of lives), the audience was never in doubt for an instant that he was innocent of all charges.

In most series the immediate surroundings, or "set," reflect the total world of the characters: the kitchen of Edith Bunker, the living room of Lucy Ricardo, the kitchen of the Kramdens, the lodge hall of Kingfish, the police station in "Dragnet." The realm of the outlaw, though, usually remains vague, dark, elusive. The implication here is that once a crime is committed, there is a moral retribution that begins instantly, a form of limbo that becomes further abstracted when apprehension occurs and banishment is meted out. For Kimble, the circumstances were particularly ironic. Removed from his law-abiding context, the hospital, his "punishment" became a world where he couldn't practice his craft—a form of suspension, just short of total banishment. Suspension and banishment were the real punishments Kimble sought to escape, the motive for his relentless pursuit of the one-armed man, the "real" criminal who, ironically, could never "exchange positions" with Kimble and exist in the law-abiding world of the socially acceptable. It is this imbalance that allowed Kimble to crisscross the social borders of good and evil. The one-armed man's missing limb both limited him physically and "marked" him socially; the ironic metaphorical correlative of blind justice!

Kimble's descension (or ascension) into limbo was complex and frightening. As the good doctor, his life was essentially an unhappy and unfulfilled one—a bad marriage and a tedious professional burden. As the fugitive, it was romantic, dangerous, and ultimately redeeming. As Dr. Kimble his hair was gray, his uniform white, his life colorless. As the fugitive his hair was black, his clothes jeans and zipper jackets, his life filled with adventures. In effect, his escape into darkness was a return to his romantic, if not purely rebellious, youth, a revitalization, a second chance in more ways than one. Why not leave the country and the life of a fugitive in South America, never to be seen or heard from again? Because social condemnation was morally wrong and had to be corrected. The social responsibility of Dr. Kimble was a validation of his moral soundness, of his "innocence," the equivocator for his unbridled escape into fantasy that kept him on the edge, in pursuit of the one-armed man.

And yet, and yet, and yet. Kimble never showed any remorse over the death of his wife, the overwhelming single factor the jury used to determine his guilt. They were allowed to hear evidence that the Kimbles fought, that Dr. Kimble wanted a divorce, that Mrs. Kimble didn't. Society, then, provided a motive; the jury completed the action with its verdict. This set into motion Kimble's escape, once again the hand of fate giving and taking—giving Kimble "freedom" from his profession and his wife, taking away his opportunity to enjoy it. This give and take was further underscored by the personification of society's outrage, the relentless pursuit of the good doctor by Lieutenant Phillip Gerard, "obsessed" with the capture of Richard Kimble.

Gerard's inspired (if misguided) sense of justice forced him to share Kimble's existential dilemma of confused identities, for by pursuing Kimble he was of course pursuing, indirectly, the one-armed man whose very existence he denied. Yet, when Kimble was finally redeemed and returned to society, it was with society's approval and subsequent reward, the return to "official" identity and status, while for Lieutenant Gerard the end of the chase meant a further descent into an already private and endless hell. Kimble's redemption confirmed Gerard's "error," his pursuit of the wrong man. This transference of guilt completed the cycle, from the pursuer who is also pursued (Kimble) to the pursuer who becomes pursued by his own consuming guilt (Gerard).

Kimble's social restoration signaled the end to his claim as the ultimate romantic. Without a criminal to pursue, Gerard's future was suspended, an ironic form of "punishment" for his misguided obsession. In the end, Kimble could exist without Gerard, but Gerard couldn't survive without Kimble. The hand of fate, which altered the social norm in the name of justice, sent the main characters of this special drama into delirious pursuit of themselves, setting off forces that defined and destroyed the standard social views of right and wrong, confusing them with good and evil, constantly reversing and inverting accepted notions of social behavior in order to establish the higher priorities of personal integrity.

HOWDY DOODY: December 27, 1947–September 30, 1960,
             NBC.
Producers: Martin Stone, Roger Muir
2,543 episodes

KUKLA, FRAN AND OLLIE: November 29, 1948–August 31,
             1957, NBC/ABC.
Producers: Beulah Zachary, Burr Tillstrom
000 episodes

CAPTAIN VIDEO AND HIS VIDEO RANGERS: 1949–1956,
             Dumont.
Producers: Olga Druce, Frank Telford

ADVENTURES OF SUPERMAN: Syndicated 1951–1957.
Producers: Whitney Wellsworth, Robert J. Maxwell, Bernard
             Luber
104 episodes

**THE WONDERFUL WORLD OF DISNEY—DISNEYLAND—
WALT DISNEY PRESENTS—THE MICKEY
MOUSE CLUB: Various dates, ABC/NBC/CBS.**

CAPTAIN KANGAROO: October 3, 1955–still running, CBS.
**Producers: Peter Birch, Jon Stone, Robert Myhreim, Bob
Claver, Dave Connell, Sam Gibbon, Al Hyslop, Jack
Miller, Jim Hirschfield**

BATMAN: January 12, 1966–March 14, 1968, ABC.
Producers: Greenway Productions, Howie Horwitz
Executive Producer: William Dozier
120 episodes

SESAME STREET: November 10, 1969–still running, PBS.
Executive Producer: Jon Stone
Producer: Dulcy Singer

"Children's" shows of the fifties escaped the burgeoning medium's quest for respectability. Without the responsibility toward children later generations of shows would bear, "Howdy Doody" flourished freely, giving the first generation of TV children all those marvelous characters, puppets, surreal clowns and princesses, brought to us by Wonder bread, the original health food that helped to build strong bones first eight then twelve ways, even as Clarabelle tried to break every one in Buffalo Bob's body. Buffalo Bob (Bob Smith) dressed in buckskin and fringe, wore his hair long and had a generally irreverent attitude. He was, in fact, the first hippie, the once and future logo for the flower-power generation, the kids who would grow out of the peanut gallery after screaming, heads back, mouths wide open, "It's 'Howdy Doody' time!" Indians were good, women were princesses, clowns were always stoned. If, later on, "Sesame Street" enforced method, Doodyville first and always encouraged imagination.

"Captain Video" was that special program for children that remained as young and vigorous as its audience. Before videotape, before big budgets, before the tube was liberated from the plodding studio theatrics of "golden age" dramas, the Captain's adventures soared through the airwaves, beyond the limitations of simple "acting," beyond the stilted studio stylistics, beyond the cardboard production values. The Video Rangers were headed by the forever-fifteen Don Hastings, who led the journey through space without the obligatory excess moral baggage that future sci-fi series would carry. Al Hodge, Captain Video, was the original video father image: tall, silver-haired, deep-voiced, secure, a combination of manner and stature approaching the iconographic. His career was so strongly linked to the Captain's that both careers ended when the show was finally canceled, as did George Reeves's Superman, Bob Smith's Buffalo Bob and other TV heroes whose collective associations with their characters was always much stronger than their off-screen abilities as mortal men.

"Superman" and "Batman" share a common comic-book origin, yet as TV shows they couldn't be farther apart in concept or execution, the former a literal translation of the man of steel's physical and moral bearing, the latter a parable of the privilege of privacy, the shame of the hidden. Or, the mansion above, the bat cave below.

By the time "Batman" appeared, whimsical child's play was replaced by a cynical preference for playing at them. This series, based on the caped crusader's adventures, amounted to little more than stale video marijuana that failed to get anybody very high.

"Captain Kangaroo" cannot be criticized or condoned, just acknowledged as a product of its own longevity. Seemingly aimed at the age level of the fetus, the approach here is so gentle, so basic, so early in the morning.

One recalls fondly the gentle antics of "Kukla, Fran and Ollie" as much for Fran Allison's midwestern ethic as for her breathy mother-superior attitude toward the two pathetic, tender puppets that danced off the fingers of the reclusive Burr Tillstrom. Harmony was friendship and love of mother, a concept as American as apple pie, and about as frozen and artificially flavored. The relationship between a mother type and puppets may be more satisfying than the problematical adventures of real-life mamas and their kids on one level, but on another it becomes a demonstration of simplified whimsy rather than an expression of basic love.

The Disney influence distills to Annette's breasts, a place called Mousketeerland, and recycled films and cartoons. That Dumbo seems more frightening than "The Untouchables" isn't hard to understand once one realizes that Dumbo is also much more moving.

**MY LITTLE MARGIE: June 16, 1952–August 24, 1955,
                CBS/NBC.
Producers: Hal Roach, Jr., Roland Reed
126 episodes**

Each episode of this series began with a shot of two framed photographs—one of Margie (Gale Storm) and one of Vern Albright (Charles Farrell), Margie's father. Each picture would then come to life and explain why its occupant had a problem. Margie's was her father—a flirt, and a successful one at that. He still looked good in shorts, and just refused to "settle down." Why that was a problem for Margie wasn't made very clear, unless it was accepted that Margie, portrayed by the very adult Gale Storm, was in fact still a child, a hyperactive one at that, filled with an endless premenstrual energy. The child in all of us gathered into one of us was Storm's brilliant interpretation of the hummingbird-heartbeat Margie—a portrayal beyond the funny, into the fascinating. Her problem was very real, very Freudian: a resentment of her father's womanizing, wishing he would settle down with one woman, namely, Margie.

Vern had his own problem. "When Margie was small I could spank her and make her mind me. I had control over her. When she disobeyed I could take her roller skates away for a week."

Mrs. Odetts (Gertrude Hoffman) was the eighty-three-year-old neighbor who "baby-sat" for Margie. Hoffman's portrayal established one of the more despicable television clichés: old people portrayed as little children. Mrs. Odetts was a little child in the guise of an old woman, making her and Margie perfect "playmates," allowing for the endless "adventures" they shared as they ran around their rather large playhouse, the Carlton Arms Hotel.

Another of Margie's playmates was her boyfriend Freddie Wilson (Don Hayden), whose relationship with the little fireball anticipated Charlie Brown's with Lucy. Willie Best made an occasional appearance as Charlie, the elevator operator whose main purpose here seemed to be to contradict the wit and sophistication of the brilliant "Amos and Andy" series. Best, reduced to feet-do-your-thing routines, was simply paying collective dues in a medium dominated in the fifties (as it still is in the eighties) by middle-class, urban, white, corporate network honchos.

The expressive fifties absurdity of "My Little Margie" eventually gave way to the calculated seventies' obnoxiousness of "Mork and Mindy." Whereas Margie was sweet, energized and quite physical, Mork (Robin Williams) was stagnant, jaded, and overly articulated. Margie's joyous reaching out became Mork's muggish bullying.

OUR MISS BROOKS: October 3, 1952–September 21, 1956, CBS.
Executive Producers: Desilu, Ozzie Nelson
Producer: Larry Berns
127 episodes

"Our Miss Brooks," based on the radio series of the forties, became another highly successful Desilu production, coming out of the Desi Arnaz factory and utilizing the innovative three-camera live-on-film technique he originated with "I Love Lucy."

Eve Arden's witty portrayal of Miss Brooks allowed the high-school teacher to attain a balance between her acerbic viewpoint and her sarcastic expressiveness, offering a character void of the dowdiness of spinsterism if also denied the heat of the tin roof. Miss Brooks was the collective big-sister authority symbol for a generation of kids who received their education under the desk, out of fear of being blown to bits in a nuclear attack.

If Miss Brooks was the buffer between the adolescent agonies of her students and the ancient apathies of their principal, Mr. Conklin (Gale Gordon), she participated in, rather than refrained

from, her own reenacted school days as she pursued a piece of
her own rock; Philip Boynton (Robert Rockwell), biology instruc-
tor. Her amorous adventures put her more on the side of the
students than the authorities giving her and us a decidedly youthful point of view; an on-the-scene glimpse at the pre-*Grease* teens
of the fifties before being congealed into revisionist memories of
the seventies. If no one, including Miss Brooks, was particularly
concerned with education, no one seemed to care that no one
cared. At least there weren't any missionaries in mathematics, as
there would be later on, in "Room 222."

PRIVATE SECRETARY: September 12, 1954–September
                10, 1957, CBS/NBC.
Producer: Jack Chertok
104 episodes

"Private Secretary" starred Ann Sothern as Susie MacNamara,
a woman who wanted a career even if it meant risking spinsterism
as part of the "penalty." Susie's comrade was the switchboard
operator Vi (Ann Tyrrell), another homely put-to-work female
unfortunate who couldn't get a man to do the work for her.

Vi kept Susie informed on just about every breath their boss,
Mr. Sands (Don Porter), took, further drawing the lines of battle
between the sexes in "metropolitan" New York. On the male
side, the troops were headed by Sands, a theatrical agent who
kept Susie around, although she obviously the most incompetent secretary in the city and always put a hitch in his make-out
plans. The touchy, if provocative situation of having an affair
with your secretary while living the gay bachelor life was side-
stepped, not by lack of opportunity as much as lack of good
writing.

Plots suffered from several sitcom cliché pitfalls, including the
abrupt character-change-as-resolution. A sponsor is outraged by
some foul-up that would, in any other situation, cause Sands's
relationship with his client to collapse and his head to roll. However, much to the surprise of everyone involved (except, of
course, Susie), the blunder turns out to be a blessing in disguise,
and everyone winds up laughing. Even Susie, who doesn't mind

the credit going to Mr. Sands, even though it was she who really deserved it. The final shot shows everyone standing around, hysterical with laughter. End of conflict. End of episode. End of series.

FATHER KNOWS BEST: October 3, 1954–April 5, 1963, CBS/NBC.
Producers: Eugene Rodney, Robert Young
203 episodes

This series began on radio, where it ran for five years before its nine-year network TV run. Like other long-running family series, the attraction for the viewer was as much the fascination with the real lives of the actors as with the lives of the characters they portrayed. It's difficult, if not impossible, to think about "Father Knows Best" without remembering the physical changes of the members of the family. Watching Kitten "grow up before our eyes" was also watching Lauren Chapin grow up; following Bud through his adolescence was also watching Billy Gray through his. The physical, emotional, and intellectual changes were so telescoped that we all but lost sight of, if not interest in, the lives of the fictional characters on the show in favor of the opportunity to watch the life process for real, as if the actors were photographed by some special time-lapse photography. The longer the run of the show, the more obsessively involving this experience became. The movies do the same thing, but the characters the actors portray change from film to film, so that there is a rationale for the growth and change of the real actors, separate from the roles they play. In long-run family sitcoms, the melding of actor and character is unique and electrifying. Especially when viewed in daily syndication re-runs.

Few may recall any specific episode of "Father Knows Best" because the format was so rigid, the episodes so much alike: a crisis in the life of a member of the family resolved by the brow-wrinkled, patched-sleeve wisdom of Father, who specialized in speaking softly and carrying no stick of any kind.

There were cracks, though, in the seemingly hallowed halls of the Anderson household. For one thing, no one had any sense of humor; small problems became "crises," adding greater weight to the "wisdom" of Jim Anderson (Robert Young), more holy than wholesome, whose unimaginative common sense masqueraded as middle-American "wisdom." Further, the whole town of Springfield, Somewhere, U.S.A., seemed devoid of the American spirit so valued in this "typical" family. No baseball, basketball or football teams. No industry, slums, minorities. No bars, no crime, just plenty of insurance policies and patched-sleeve men who sold them. Yet, the acceptance of this show was so complete that the federal government "took over" Springfield once to make a Treasury Department propaganda film involving the Andersons in a threatened takeover of the United States by a fascist dictator!

The "Father Knows Best" formula was one of substitution and bypass. There was a lack of emotion running through the entire family that came across as respectability; a sense of restraint passed for real love; posturing and smiling sufficed in place of real compassion. This well-coordinated formality was best epitomized by Jim Anderson, apropriately stoic, always seeming to say things importantly, even if what he said wasn't all that important.

THE ADVENTURES OF OZZIE AND HARRIET: October 3, 1952–September 3, 1966, ABC.
Producers: Ozzie Nelson, Robert Angus, Bill Lewis, Leo Penn
435 episodes

Ozzie Nelson, along with Desi Arnaz and Jackie Gleason, was one of the pioneers of American TV situation comedy. A triple threat, he wrote, produced and directed his fourteen-year family series on television, following several years on the radio.

Once again the situation here is one of interest in the real lives of the actors portraying characters as much as it is with the "lives" of the TV characters, but with a difference, for "Ozzie and Harriet" twists Pirandello: the real lives of the actors are the same lives as the characters they portray, the TV family is in fact a real family. Time is shared between actor, person, work and life. And the audience, of course.

The Nelsons let it all hang out, California style. The groovy old

man, Ozzie, endeared himself to us for the very reasons that Jim
Anderson ("Father Knows Best") couldn't. While Anderson
seemed to know all the answers, he lacked the passion to make it
matter. While Ozzie knew none of the answers, his stuttering
search for solutions reflected his willingness to try to work it out.
The Nelsons understood this and said, Hey, pop, there are no real
"problems," only "situations"; therefore, no solutions, only
choices.

If nothing ever "happened" in the Nelson home, it was because nothing was ever serious enough to require formal resolution. Perhaps the greatest difference between the Nelsons and the
Andersons was that living in Middle-America made "wishing" a
family pastime, while hanging out in L.A. made dreaming a way
of life.

For the record, Ozzie Nelson did have a job. He was the
producer of "The Adventures of Ozzie and Harriet."

MAKE ROOM FOR DADDY: September 29, 1953–September
                          14, 1964, ABC/CBS.
Executive Producer: Danny Thomas, Sheldon Leonard
336 episodes

If "Father Knows Best" retained the myth of "nothing ever
changes, families stay together forever," "Make Room for
Daddy" suggested that families were constantly changing, adapt-
ing to one crisis after another, sometimes breaking up as a result.
This show is the only one in which a character, after having been
established and featured for four years—Margaret Williams (Jean
Hagen), Danny Williams' (Danny Thomas) wife—"dies" (until
the much publicized death of Edith Bunker in the fall 1980 episode
of "Archie Bunker's Place." Edith's death, though, is part of a
larger format change; out of the Bunker household into the Bunker
bar. Hence it becomes a qualified "death" in the family).

Death on TV means separation. Usually we know little about
the peripheral, one-shot characters who make an entrance and die
(as in "Maude" and "All in the Family" episodes), and even less
about the cause of death. When Margaret Williams died, however,
we never found out how or why. She just disappeared and was

replaced by Danny's second wife, who in turn became a continuation of his first, making no contribution, therefore no change, to Danny's lifestyle, to Danny's life.

Danny Williams was a nightclub entertainer in New York whose career was in direct conflict with his somewhat less-than-successful role of father. This premise figured most heavily in the relationship between Danny and his son Rusty (Rusty Hamer), the only boy in an otherwise female household. The growing hostility between father and son was viewed cynically; the physical resemblance between Rusty and Danny turned on a post of fear and outrage as the youngster found himself looking and acting more and more like the father he was growing to resent.

Danny Williams, seemingly part Lebanese, Italian, Jewish, and black, epitomized middle-aged American fathers confronting the erosion of their youth by surrendering custom suits and dollar cigars for jeans and marijuana. The problem, though, is that by the time they get the courage to wear sideburns, they have to dye them black.

**ETHEL AND ALBERT: April 25, 1953–July 6, 1956,
                NBC/ABC/CBS.**
Producers: Thomas Loeb, Walter Hart
Various live and filmed formats/episodes

Ethel and Albert (Peg Lynch and Alan Bunce), unhappily married, traded one-liners rather than kisses. Theirs was a strange world, filled with reminders of their failed marriage. Gadgets in the household continually broke down at the most inopportune moments, creating a cacophony of sounds and sights that seemed to stress the strained unworkability of their shared lives. This idea was further advanced by the absence of children and the presence of a nagging aunt (Margaret Hamilton), whose snide negativism added unneeded weight to the already heavy situation.

This stylized middle-aged, middle-American breakdown was a nifty use of technical tactics in the absence of genuine style. Here the relentless unfunny one-liners became a statement of dramatic irony rather than simply an attempt at getting laughs.

TOPPER: October 9, 1953–September 30, 1955, CBS.
Producers: John W. Loveton, Bernard L. Schubert
78 episodes

"Topper" represents a peculiar sub-genre of TV sitcoms, the ghost story. The reason why few succeeded and none is memorable is because television is already a medium of "ghosts." Performers drift from show to show assuming new characters and new lives; stars of long-running programs exist in a world where their static adventures become, in effect, a living disclaimer to the natural-life process of change and development. The appearance of spirits and alter egos is redundant within the structure of situation comedy.

Because television mythifies death, ghosts, rather than having escaped the human condition, become, in fact, an extension of it, have Topper (Leo G. Carroll) not be haunted but merely aging, and the tables decidedly turn toward the social/realistic, away from the metaphysical/fantastic.

MEDIC: September 13, 1954–November 19, 1956, NBC.
Executive Producer: Worthington Miner
Producers: Frank LaTourette, James Moser
59 episodes

The medical cycle lasted three generations on network television: the "Medic" era, the "Kildare/Casey" era, and the "Welby" era.

"Medic" introduced Richard Boon as Dr. Styner, occasional star and regular narrator of the anthology series shot on location at various hospitals in and around Los Angeles, supplementing the acting cast with working doctors and nurses. This device added to the authentic look of the stories, and also bolstered TV's already heavily reverential attitude toward the medical profession. Doctors were missionaries; hospitals, sanctuaries; victims at the mercy of the gods. As Styner would put it at the start of each week's episode, doctors of medicine were the "Guardians of birth, healers of the sick, and comforters of the aged."

The problem, then, was how conflict, could rear its ugly, if dramatically secular, head. "Medic" relied on the blood and gore of the operating room, without implying the amputation of evil. Instead, shock value and fear were incorporated into the fascination and exploration so that the sight of blood became a moment of drama exclusive of whose blood it was, or whose guts were at stake. "Medic" was a scrub opera without personification for its implied conflicts.

GUNSMOKE: September 10, 1955–September 1, 1975, CBS.
Producers: Norman MacDonnell, Philip Leacock, Edgar
**   Peterson, John Mantley**
633 episodes (400 one-hour, 233 half-hour)

"Gunsmoke" was the longest-running dramatic series on television, beginning as a half-hour show, eventually expanding to one hour. Among the first programs to shed TV's eastern-intellectual-theatrical association in favor of a western-action-cinematic motif, "Gunsmoke" was TV's first "adult Western." CBS vigorously pursued John Wayne to star in the series. He declined, offering the marshal's badge to James Arness, Wayne's personal choice to portray Marshal Matt Dillon of Dodge City.

Matt Dillon represented the patriotic ethos of the American conservative: upright, tall, silent, manly, capable of taming the Wild West. If Wayne represented hard-linism in his movies, Arness was his video counterpart. After the violent gunfights of "Gunsmoke" were curbed in the wake of sixties revisionist attitudes toward "excessive" violence on the air, Arness simply shifted from six guns to two fists as metaphoric extensions of integrity; the long arm of the law.

The supporting cast of "Gunsmoke" was deliberately chosen to serve the Arness persona. Arness, six-foot-seven, towered over his under-six-foot costars.

Kitty (Amanda Blake), "hostess" of the town saloon, was in reality the town whore; "friend" but never lover of the marshal. Their relationship remained only slightly lurid, even so it still approached the limits of the tube's allowance. Matt, then, was Kitty's knight in shining armor, Kitty doing double duty as mother and sister. Her saloon was also her moral prison, guarded by Matt Dillon as carefully as he guarded the other jailhouse of Dodge City. Kitty's extreme popularity as a character on the long-running series was due in large part to Americans' fascination with—attraction and repulsion to—hookers, especially those in madonna clothes. Kitty's was a case of officially sanctioned lust.

Doc (Milburn Stone) was a medical missionary whose contribution was wisdom, assistance and common sense, the tools he used to keep Matt alive. Doc removed countless bullets from the marshal's shoulders, legs, chest, arms and back in order to keep him in prime fighting condition—in effect, maintaining the social order by maintaining Matt's heartbeat.

And, of course, there was Chester (Dennis Weaver), TV's first legitimate cult hero, limping his way into pre-Fonzie national preoccupation. If he represented the weak side of the otherwise towering marshal, he also represented the notion of the timid innocent who believes in the need for protection by an almighty enforcer.

As Dillon aged, and physical violence gave way to a battle of wits, Dillon's continual never-ending attempts to preserve law and order in the Wild West were also his attempts to stop the inevitable march of time. One could almost see a jeep pulling up in the distance. Dillon's approaching old age was a concession to his inability to accept the twentieth century. The effect was triple: the decline of the sheriff, the decline of the Old West, and the decline of the series, as the commercially ageist CBS newtwork refused to open its lens aperture to shoot into any sunset.

YOU'LL NEVER GET RICH: September 20, 1955–September 11, 1959, CBS.
Executive Producer: Edward J. Montagne
Producer: Aaron Ruben
138 episodes

Created by Nat Hiken, "Bilko" (as the show was popularly known) tagged the peacetime army-life experience as a gathering place for the collective adolescent spirit, where the haves and the have-nots are equalized and put to the test. Those who can, take from those who have. Bilko (Phil Silvers) headed a platoon that was closer to a street gang, with Colonel Hall (Paul Ford) their collective father figure trying to contain them. Bilko had no real talent and correctly perceived that for those without special qualities, living is reduced to existing from scam to scam. And he acted accordingly.

His gang members included Harvey Lembeck, Joe E. Ross and Maurice Gosfield—all short, stocky, middle-aged men who'd lost their biggest turf, their youth, and were now forced to huddle together to try and make three squares and a place to sack. Bilko, taller, sleeker, quicker than the others, took on the responsibility for them by keeping them dependent on him. Bilko's army-life scam existence philosophy was simple: get the most by doing as little as possible.

Phil Silvers' performance deserves special mention. His manic lip service both justified and rationalized his actions. In this way he recalled Ralph Kramden, another scammer, except that where Kramden was blissfully innocent, Bilko was cynically corrupt.

THE HONEYMOONERS: **October 1, 1955–February, 1956, CBS.**
Executive Producer: **Jack Philbin**
Producer: **Jack Hurdle**
39 episodes

It is the original thirty-nine half-hour episodes of "The Honeymooners" that have been in syndication the past twenty-four years, and that may run another twenty-four without showing any loss in popularity as new audiences discover the devastatingly satirical day-to-day adventures of Ralph Kramden (Jackie Gleason), civil servant, working-class slave.

The "classic" stature of the series episodes—the single set, live audience, simultaneous three-camera kinescope—is as much a product of early television's pragmatic style of production as any stylistic insights on the part of Gleason and company. During its embryonic fifties, television was still unsure of its communicative definition—a medium for the transmission of data from other, outside sources, or for the origination as well as the transmission of "television."

Gleason's use of a stage with live audience and three-camera setup was derived from the Broadway-stage concept of the proscenium arch and fourth wall. Fifties television expanded the fourth-wall audience viewpoint to include not only the live audience but the one tuning in as well for use in staging sitcoms, this technique didn't originate with Gleason; Desi Arnaz introduced it in "I Love Lucy." Further, the fondly recalled "kitchen sink" atmosphere of Kramden's flat was also a matter of television practicality as much as television stylistics, the latter suggesting Kramden's bulk being even greater within cramped physical surroundings, the former a function of the limitation of early TV cameras, which required small sets and therefore limited physical actions. As videotape and film technology liberated television from the fifties' inverted-lens cameras, it also freed characters physically and stylistically, opening up the possibilities of multisets and outdoor settings. The elimination of the fourth-wall set gave viewers, in a sense, another viewpoint as well as another view.

However, "The Honeymooners" isn't remembered because of, or in spite of, sets, camera techniques, or studio limitations, but for its relentless investigation of Kramden's working-class plight. A visit to Kramden's kitchen became an invitation to examine Ralph's angst: the public servant who wanted to be the king of his castle, to rule with an iron fist. Revolutions have sprung from less.

"The Honeymooners" was loosely based on an old Laurel and Hardy feature, "The Sons of the Desert," the saga of two married men constantly trying and failing to outwit their wives in the name of male-exclusive fun. Gleason combined the Laurel and Hardy comic spirit with the memory of his own unfunny Brooklyn working-class childhood to create Ralph Kramden, good buddy Ed Norton (Art Carney), and the wives, Alice (Audrey Meadows) and Trixie (Joyce Randolph).

Kramden's world was defined by lack of money, lack of decent job, lack of opportunity, and finally lack of ego. His excessive blustering and ranting at his wife and best friend Norton were charged with an ironic fuel, for if Ralph's boisterousness was a defensive mask for his feelings of inadequacy, it was the sensitive Ralph beneath the mask that Alice sought. Norton, more accepting of his lower-class existence—he worked in the city's sewer system!—was gifted with a common sense that often made Ralph seem foolish, even as Norton's lean body often made Ralph feel fatter. Most times it was Norton, not Ralph, who got the last laugh, and at Ralph's emotional expense. When all else failed, a crack about Ralph's weight could do it, underscoring Ralph's frustrations at having huge mass without great stature.

Alice also taunted Ralph about his weight, serving to diminish his self-image while constantly pricking at his fat. The implication was clear: she wouldn't go to bed with him because she *couldn't* go to bed with him. As stated by Alice in response to Ralph's reminding her that if he left she couldn't put her arms around a memory, Alice dispassionately retorted, "I can't even put my arms around you." Yet neither Alice nor Norton made any real effort to help Ralph reduce. Oh, one time Alice tried to put him on a diet, but without the necessary emotional support needed for an undertaking of that size, both she and Ralph failed. It was almost as if Alice wanted to keep Ralph overweight, therefore unappealing to other women, other temptations, or greater success at his job—the latter especially a threat to the security of her home, such as it was. Better to have a fat, faithful daydreamer than a thin, never-at-home, promiscuous achiever. And Norton, he always managed to eat huge amounts of tasty, nasty foods under the alerted nose of the woesome Ralph without ever gaining so much as an ounce. Ralph's inability to cope with his weight problem underscored his inability to rise above his minimal existence. It served more often than not to reduce his inspirations to the failed levels of his friends and loved one, rather than allowing him to bring their lives into the grander realm of his own, if imagined, stature.

"The Honeymooners" was one of the few situation comedies to deal with the subject of money—the lack of which, Ralph figured, was surely the reason he had so many problems he couldn't solve. His shortage of funds and subsequent confusion about his own self-worth was a basic premise for the series. Ralph's working-class psyche was picked over relentlessly.

Money, like sex, was an elusive carrot never to be had, obsessions driven by lack rather than excess.

Gleason resurrected "The Honeymooners" many times after the 1955–56 season, but was never again able to achieve the delicate balance between pathos and ethos that made the original thirty-nine episodes so special. Eventually, Ralph was allowed to achieve success and some money, which all but destroyed the original premise of the show. Gleason retired to Florida, and Ralph was reduced to sunstroked one-liners. "The Honeymooners" had been one of the few situation comedies to draw its humor from situations rather than one-liners. When quips were all that remained, the honeymoon ended.

ALFRED HITCHCOCK PRESENTS: October 2,
                          1955–September 6, 1965, CBS/NBC.
Executive Producer: Alfred Hitchcock, MCA
Producers: Joan Harrison, Shamley Productions
360 episodes

Alfred Hitchcock is a tremendously complex subject; his work in television becomes, by comparison, a footnote to his celebrated movie career. He was the only major Hollywood director to work actively, in continuing series form, on television. His participation, from the beginning, was more than producer and host. He directed nearly twenty episodes, including the famous "Lamb to Slaughter" vignette in which Barbara Bel Geddes (a favorite 1950s Hitchcock heroine) murders her policeman husband as he threatens to leave her for another woman. The Hitchcock touches abound; the victim is a policeman, a figure of power and menace in the Hitchcock tradition, and the murderer is a gentle-looking, pregnant mama-to-be. The murder is set up so that the audience feels compassion for the predator and a sense of satisfaction at the moment of violence that causes the policeman's death. Thus, by implicating the audience in the murder, Hitchcock set up a situation for the second act wherein the audience hopes the woman won't get caught. The solution— having her cook the murder weapon, a frozen leg of lamb—is made even more ironic by the fact that the investigating squad joins her for dinner. The final bit of dialogue has the head of the investigation munching on a piece of lamb and remarking that he is sure the solution to the murder is right under their noses. The last shot is Bel Geddes' face, slowly moving from stiff indifference to sly grin, anticipating the last moments of the 1961 Hitchcock feature *Psycho*.

Plagued with censorship squabbles throughout the run of the series, Hitchcock was forced to assure audiences the aspects of law and order his shows rendered foolish and trivial were in fact still in control. At the end of "Lamb to Slaughter" Hitchcock informed the audience that the woman remarried, and the same situation happened to her again—suggesting perhaps that she drove her men to other women—and that when she attempted to kill her second husband she didn't succeed because they had forgotten to pay their gas and electric bill, resulting in the freezer being turned off, the leg of lamb unfrozen and soft, the murder only attempted, the victim spared, the killer apprehended.

The late fifties to mid-sixties span that Hitchcock spent in television, parallel an interesting period of his film career. The show began about the same time his feature film *The Trouble with Harry* was being completed. This wide-screen, technicolor film was followed by *The Man Who Knew Too Much*, *The Wrong Man*, *Vertigo*, *North By Northwest*, *Psycho*, *The Birds*, and *Marnie*. With the exception of *Psycho*, all these films were wide-screen, color, big-budget items, forming an interesting dialectic between Hitchcock's film and TV work; between the extravagant and the spare, between those characters caught in a world overly self-indulgent, and one in which the nightmarish self was reduced to a minimum.

The movie *Psycho* may, in fact, be referred to in many ways as Hitchcock's TV cinematic realization of his well-developed TV technique. The black-and-white, spare settings, the fast cutting, the emphasis on medium shots and close-ups, the episodic nature of the three "acts" of *Psycho* (the murder of Marion, the murder of Arbogast, the capture of Norman) and the postscript (the "explanation" by the psychiatrist) reflect the tight structure of television brought to delirious limits. Perhaps Hitchcock's eagerness to work in television was prompted by its structural rigidity which, in many ways, reflected his own highly structured film stylistics, for Hitchcock's movies brilliantly stressed restriction as theme as well as format.

LOVE THAT BOB: **January 2, 1955–September 15, 1959, NBC/CBS.**
Producer: **Paul Henning**
173 episodes

A young, good-looking bachelor loves to chase women so much he turns his obsession into a career; he photographs them as a way to romance them, and he romances them as a way to photograph them. Sound like something on the drawing board for the TV sitcom schedule of 1985? Try a sitcom from the fifties, starring the improbable Bob Cummings in what was one of the cleverest, funniest shows of that decade, perhaps in all of TV history.

By 1955 the sitcom format was so rigidly structured it was difficult to sell something new to the networks. Everyone loved a "Lucy," domesticity with a daffy husband and a couple of neighbors. Or a "Father Knows Best" with daddy having a direct line to Heaven, the family molded out of Protestant Ethic clay. So it was all the more startling to see just how far Cummings & Co. could go within the bounds of the obligatory.

If Bob's world was a bachelor paradise, he still had, necessarily, a "family." Rosemary DeCamp was his "sister," although it was obvious she was really more wife than sibling. Bob was constantly "hiding" his romances from her, leaving through the back door to avoid being "caught." His "nephew" (Dwayne Hickman) was more like a son, even though he looked a lot like "Uncle" Bob and shared his obsessive desire for beautiful women, if not his ability to get them. Rounding out the "family" was Schultzy (Ann B. Davis), Bob's "secretary," who captured the cynicism of all the homelies who secretly lust after their handsome bosses, and who accept their own unattractive "looks" as the reason they fail to romance them.

Contrast this 1950s feminine myth with the 1970s notion that women require a degree in police work, or superwomb capabilities, or the surrender of romance in the name of career in order to score. Take the newsroom where Mary Richards (Mary Tyler Moore) worked, where sexuality had no bargaining power, and sex was no bargain. Mary was no Shirley Swanson (Joi Lansing), Bob's favorite "model," who found happiness disrobing and posing. And Shirley was for sure no Mary who longed to find happiness with a man, any man, but who didn't have a clue as to how to go about it.

Bob's amorous adventures brought him closer to the altar than he ever wanted to get. Marriage scared him to death. His "close calls" reminded him, and us, of the chilly underside to Bob's womanizing—the icy fear of intimacy that pushed him to keep the fever high just to stay alive.

WAGON TRAIN: September 18, 1957–September 5, 1965,
**   NBC/ABC.**
Executive Producer: Howard Christie
442 episodes

Loosely derived from *The Canterbury Tales,* "Wagon Train" brought us, each TV season, from St. Louis to California by covered wagon. Each week's episode highlighted a different family traveling on the train. Ward Bond as the wagonmaster demonstrated strength and maturity as the leader of the pack. The stylistics here were derived from John Ford's indelible Western imagery compounded by the long, breathtaking vista of the human chain-link stretching the bounds of humanity across the frontier land. Ford, in fact, directed one episode of the series.

Ward Bond (a favorite John Ford actor) was able to evoke the qualities of compassion and leadership as he supervised the season-long treks; there was always someplace left behind, and someplace else just beyond the horizon. An intelligent, often moving series, "Wagon Train," was another nail in the coffin of the early, exotic childlike TV Westerns such as "The Lone Ranger," "Hopalong Cassidy," "Roy Rogers" and "Gene Autry," six-gun glitter heroes of the horse operas' first generation, whose antic shoot-em-ups nevertheless helped the genre to escape its own arrested adolescence in favor of adulthood in TV's vast westland.

PERRY MASON: September 21, 1957–September 4, 1966, CBS.
Executive Producers: Arthur Marks, Gail Patrick Jackson
Producers: Art Seid, Sam White, Ben Brady
271 episodes

THE DEFENDERS: September 16, 1961–September 9,
1965, CBS.
Producers: Herbert Brodkin, Robert Maxwell, Kenneth Utt
132 episodes

EAST SIDE, WEST SIDE: September 23, 1963–September 14,
1964, CBS.
Producers: David Susskind, Don Kranze, Arnold Perl, Larry
Arrick
26 episodes

IRONSIDE: September 14, 1967–January 16, 1975, NBC.
Executive Producers: Joel Rogosin, Cy Chermak
Producers: Norman Jolley, Frank Price, Douglas Benton
120 episodes

LOU GRANT: September 20, 1977–still running, CBS.
Executive Producers: Allan Burns, James L. Brooks, Gene
Reynolds
Producer: Gene Reynolds

Both "Lou Grant" and "East Side, West Side" fail as drama
and therefore as effective social statement. Substituting diatribe
for dialogue, these shows managed to replace conflict with de-
bate. The problem was point of view or the lack of it. Too strong a
position risks offending large numbers of viewers. The reluctance
to take a stand redefines social integrity (for TV producers)
as middle-of-the-roadism, a perverse radicalism disguised as
moderation. This illusion of moderation usually brings a comple-
mentary lack of passion to dramatic works, as in the case of "Lou

Grant" (Ed Asner), managing editor for a post-Watergate news-paper whose reporting style is seemingly always undercover, with the "story" the basis for moral posturing. Dog bites man is news if there's a socially relevant reason why, and don't worry, Lou's people will search for it until they find it.

Lou Grant certainly gained respect for doing eight years with good old Mary and never laying a hand on her (as the next-to-last episode of "The Mary Tyler Moore Show" assured us). For that alone he deserves unlimited reverence. Lou's "heroic" disregard for formal authority might seem a minor point to consider unless examined in terms of his overall reluctance to commit himself to any situation, including a sexual one. This is the only apparent link between Lou Grant of "The Mary Tyler Moore Show," a grumpy, beer-drinking, grossly overweight "guy," and the active, polite, restrained, witty, sensitive Lou Grant of newspaper fame. Some men find God after forty. Lou went one step better and became God. The problem was that Lou's halo blended in all too well with the others in the newsroom, like so many candy canes on a Christmas tree. Old Lou expressed his morality through a continual striving, a naturally dramatic context. New Lou dis-played his morality after the fact, by virtue of achievement, not nearly as dramatic or effective.

"The Defenders" anticipated Lou Grant's reverence, this time in the courtroom, where lawyers always upheld the law regard-less of their client's ability to pay. The real action, as anyone who's ever dealt with lawyers knows, is heightened by their human limitation, not weakened by it.

"Perry Mason" was another victim of this mythic morality represented by the social/noble genre of TV series. We were virtually assured that Mason would win his case at the end of each and every episode. This not only robbed the district attorney of a winning record, it also deprived the audience of any sem-blance of drama. The guilty parties usually confessed from the public pews, suggesting that the destiny of all criminals is confes-sion, either directly through prosecution, or indirectly through the eroding of one's evil will by the collective moral conscience.

Perry Mason was portrayed by Raymond Burr, who continued his television career in yet another annoying series, "Ironside," in which he played the role of a detective confined to a wheelchair, further reducing his (Burr's) already minimal physicality. The show exploited the trauma and tragedy of the paraplegic/quadraplegic experience. Ironside was shot by a criminal in the opening moments of the first episode and was thereafter confined to a wheelchair as he sought to rid the world of crime. The show inflicted a false sense of stature on the chair-bound hero by omitting a crucial step. It was quite impossible to experience, and subsequently feel for Ironside's fall from grace, not having known him well enough before that fall.

MAVERICK: September 22, 1957–July 8, 1962, ABC.
Producers: Roy Huggins, William L. Stewart
124 episodes

THE RESTLESS GUN: September 23, 1957–September 14, 1959, NBC.
Producers: John Payne, David Dortort
77 episodes

WANTED—DEAD OR ALIVE: September 6, 1958–March 29, 1961, CBS.
Producers: John Robinson, Ed Adamson, Harry Harris
94 episodes

THE RIFLEMAN: September 30, 1958–July 1, 1963, ABC.
Producers: Jules Levy, Arthur Gardner, Arnold Laven
168 episodes

RAWHIDE: January 9, 1959–January 4, 1966, CBS.
Producers: Charles Warren, Endre Bohem, Vincent M. Fennelly
144 episodes

BONANZA: September 12, 1959–January 16, 1973, NBC.
Producers: Richard Collins, David Dortort, Robert Blees
440 episodes

HOTEL DE PAREE: October 2, 1959–September 23, 1960, CBS.
Producer: Stanley Rubin
33 episodes

THE REBEL: October 4, 1959–September 17, 1961, ABC.
Producer: Andrew J. Fenady
76 episodes

KUNG FU: October 1, 1972–June 28, 1975, ABC.
Producer: Jerry Thorpe
72 episodes

The above Westerns are noted for the following reasons:

"The Restless Gun," starring John Payne, offered an excellent portrait of an aging, slightly over-the-hill cowboy, particularly moving in light of Payne's then-declining Hollywood movie career. Taking hold of the production reins, Payne rotated "The Restless Gun" toward the semiautobiographical, a panoramic metaphor for the last days of the Old West, the Old Hollywood, the Old Movie Stars.

"Maverick" gave us the first look at James Garner's attractive brand of sarcasm. Garner's career on the show came to a premature end because of a contract dispute similar to the one Clint Walker found himself involved in with the "Rawhide" series. "Rawhide" also gave viewers their first look at Clint Eastwood, a decided plus, but not enough to outweigh the remaining minuses. "Wagon Train" explored the movement of humanity searching for a better life. The chief protagonists in "Rawhide" were cattle.

"Hotel de Paree" defined heroism as yet another reward for redemption, as it rewrote history to make The Sundance Kid an ex-con who'd done time in prison for the accidental killing of another man, "Accidental" the escape valve allowing for redemption. Sundance's penance was a stint in limbo, guardian for, but not privy to, the "European" boardinghouse, a.k.a. Parisian whorehouse.

"Wanted—Dead or Alive" elevated Steve McQueen to star status, the pouting airwave equivalent of James Dean. "The Rebel" gave us a brief glimpse at the neurotic Nick Adams, the little-man hero anticipating the little-man movie syndrome of the Dustin Hoffman sixties and seventies. "Daniel Boone" was a hugely successful if woefully intermittent sendup of Fess Parker's original TV burst as Davy Crockett. "The Rifleman" offered a motherless child with an overcompensating father (good characters, weak dramatic combination) corrected by "Bonanza," which offered three motherless children and an overcompensating father (good characters, better dramatic combination). "The Big Valley" further complicated the family saga, this time with Barbara Stanwyck in the role of the overcompensating mother (good characters, best dramatic combination).

"The Wild Wild West" was little more than a trashy ripoff of the James Bond movie cycle; "Kung Fu," an even trashier ripoff of Quinn Martin's "The Fugitive." For all its Eastern-mystic double-talk, "Kung Fu" never came close to the pure mysticism guiding the plight of Dr. Richard Kimble. The only good thing to be said about the atrocious "Kung Fu" is that it made "The Fugitive" that much greater by comparison.

77 SUNSET STRIP: October 10, 1958–September 9, 1964, ABC.
Producers: William T. Orr, Roy Huggins, William Conrad,
** Howie Horwitz, Fenton Earnshaw**
225 episodes

"77 Sunset Strip" was the first serious attempt by ABC to compete with the other networks for ratings and big-dollar advertising revenues. Having the least to lose, ABC moved first to shed the eastern-theatrical image of fifties' dramatic TV fare, going west to the moribund movie-studio back lots to coproduce and finance action series. "Strip" was among the first such series to dwell on the night side of Hollywood life, the pre-cocaine/marijuana heroism/hedonism trip on the streets of El Lay.

If any major dramatic defect can be found in the plethora of action/adventure/detective series that followed "77 Sunset Strip," it was the easy surrender to action as a pretext for, rather than an extension of, motivations. Criminals were neither sociologically nor philosophically motivated; they just did bad things. They lusted for money, they hated police, and they were easy targets for two-dimensional detective/heroes to do battle against.

Most viewers first recall Edd "Kookie" Burns when they think of "77 Sunset Strip," and with good reason. His presence was utilized to sell the show the way a pop song utilizes a melody as a hook to establish a pretty, familiar chorus between verses. If Stu Bailey (Efrem Zimbalist, Jr.) and Jeff Spencer (Roger Smith) were verse, Kookie was decidedly chorus, familiar and attractive between gunshots.

TV "craze" personalities remain in the memory more for their characteristics than for their characterizations. Fonzie's leather jacket and thumbs, Suzanne's breasts, Farrah's hair (she merely borrowed Kookie's comb, that's all).

NAKED CITY: September 30, 1958–September 11, 1963, ABC.
Producer: ABC
138 episodes (99 one-hour, 39 half-hour)

I LED THREE LIVES: 1953–1956. Syndicated.
116 episodes

TIGHTROPE!:   September 8, 1959–September 13, 1960, CBS.
Producers: Clarence Greene, Russell Rouse
37 episodes

N.Y.P.D.:   September 5, 1967–September 16, 1969, ABC.
Producer: Robert Butler
62 episodes

M SQUAD: September 20, 1957–September 13, 1960, NBC.
Producer: Lee Marvin
81 episodes

BANACEK: (NBC Wednesday Mystery Movie Segment)
                     September 13, 1972–September 3, 1974, NBC.
Producer: NBC
16 episodes

CHARLIE'S ANGELS: September 22, 1976–1981, ABC.
Executive Producer: Aaron Spelling, Leonard Goldberg
Producer: Rick Huskey, David Levinson, Barney Rosenzweig

   Both "I Led Three Lives" (syndicated) and "Tightrope" presented heroes with no clearly defined moral core. Herbert Philbrick (Richard Carlson), triple counterspy for the FBI was a virtual walking jangle of paranoia and ambivalence whose personal identity was finally subordinated in favor of the government's "cause." Successful during the McCarthy era of the fifties, the show pointedly reflected the widespread fear and malevolence that served those with power by helping to intimidate those without.
   As the decade eased up a bit in its political paranoia, the authoritarian Philbrick was replaced by the otherwise nameless "Nick" (Mike Conners) of "Tightrope." "Nick" lived on the edge, or on the wire, as it were. While Philbrick did his thing for the good of mankind, "Nick" did it, presumably, because it felt good.
   "Naked City" and "N.Y.P.D." were New York-based (and -produced) police dramas with screeching brakes and fast turns stylistically signaling danger "just around the corner." New York, like Chicago, was well suited as a physical context for the implicit middle-class fear of the inner city, setting the stage for the hi-test heroics of the city cops in "Naked City" and "N.Y.P.D.," and the homicide hierarchy of lieutenant Frank

Ballinger (Lee Marvin) of the Chicago-based "M Squad," the latter a combination of the icy L.A. paranoia of "Dragnet's" Joe Friday (Jack Webb) and the cool Manhattan romanticism of "Naked City's" Detective Flint (Paul Burke).

Street detectives took a powder during the sixties as the rural situation comedies dominated. Their seventies' resurgence their brought a few new wrinkles to the genre. No longer living in the dark, on cold city streets, these new TV cops were urbane, suave, wealthy beyond reason, West Coast cool, and intelligent: pursuing intelligent criminals, going out with intelligent girl-friends, gathering intelligent evidence, making intelligent arrests. Of all of them, the least intelligent (and most popular) was Jim Rockford (James Garner). Here, reprising aspects of his "Maverick" character, Garner emphasized his sympathetically cynical side, making him endlessly attracted to clients who "ap-peared" guilty but were, in fact, innocent. Rockford's clients, like Rockford, suffered only from coming close to the edge, not from falling over it.

"Banacek" reversed the Rockford theme. People were guilty all over the place, but appeared innocent. In fact, most of the show's crimes were committed off-camera, their solutions arrived at through long, bizarre monologues delivered by Banacek (George Peppard) at the end of each episode, a Charlie Chan recap telling us what happened, and why we couldn't figure it out before he did. The show's problem was basically structural. By reducing the audience to mere problem-solvers, dramatic involvement was suspended, resulting in a lack of interest not only in what happened, but why. "Banacek" falsely assumed there was dramatic passion in intellectual game-playing.

"Charlie's Angels" was the logical seventies progression of the triple-teaming sixties teen crime-fighting series of Aaron Spelling, including "The Rookies" and "Mod Squad." The Spelling link was further reinforced by the recurring appearance of Kate Jackson, former "Rookie's" wife, full-fledged Angel.

The thrust of Charlie's girls was spiritual, the pretty women definitely on the side of the angels. While they may occasionally have had to hit the streets to fight crime, their moral inferiors were never able to inhabit the heavenly sanctuary of Great God Charlie (John Forsythe). Interestingly, Charlie was only heard, never seen, evidence that true moral uplift comes from the sacrifice of the physical toward the spiritual. This is nice work if you can get it, and, like the Angels, you can get it if you pry.

STACCATO: September 10, 1959–September 25, 1960, NBC/ABC.
27 episodes

PETER GUNN: September 22, 1959–September 25, 1961, NBC/ABC.
Producer: Blake Edwards
114 episodes

The provocative jazz themes of Henry Mancini complemented the jazzy attitude of the suave Mr. Gunn (Craig Stevens), television's answer to Cary Grant, although no one remembers who asked the question.

TV's flirtation in the fifties with jazz as a popular musical idiom was short-lived, perhaps a response to the early radio assault of rock and roll. As musical background, jazz served to underscore the double sexual reference of Peter Gunn's name, the point made with either *Peter* or *Gunn*. However, all the jazz on the soundtrack couldn't make Gunn hip; if anything, he made the music sound square.

Gunn's hangout was a place called Mother's, the conscious Freudian irony serving here only to fog the sexual innuendos further, placing this whole affair in a precarious topheavy balance. The jazz metaphor worked much better in a less successful show, "Staccato," starring John Cassavetes in the title role.

Rather than using music to merely set the mood, Staccato's nervous, paranoid night-life existence was the natural extension of his duel careers of detective and jazz pianist, the music here a natural motif, logically filling out the aural atmosphere. Staccato's hipness was an asset; it made it easier for him to move through the shady world of those he pursued. He was a moral bounty hunter, keeping the house free from outsiders, keeping the Gunns away.

Later on, Cassavetes would exploit his nervous, improvisational attitudes in the movies where the large screen would better serve his surreal close-ups and sexual subtexts. On TV, Cassavetes came off more street rat than wild stallion, more desperate than ambitious, more relentlessly nocturnal, sorely in need of at least an occasional burst of daylight if for no other purpose than to make the darkness more fearful and the journey through it more odyssey than survival.

HAVE GUN WILL TRAVEL: September 14, 1957–September
         21, 1963, CBS.
Producers: Frank Pierson, Don Ingalls, Robert Sparks
156 episodes

BAT MASTERSON: October 8, 1958–September 21, 1961, NBC.
Producer: Andy White, Frank Pittman
108 episodes

"Bat Masterson" was one of TV's second generation cowboys, somewhere between the early six-gun and sidekick law men, and the later brooding western "heroes" of the Ponderosa. Masterson, portrayed by Gene Barry, was mythic, but with a twist. As a dandy he dressed well, spoke softly, and carried a very big stick, a thick, hard cane used to repel enemies and gain friends. If Masterson's dress was formal, his attitude was Victorian; formal dress covering primitive rage.

Masterson used his head the way Paladin (Richard Boone) did, another hybrid hero. Paladin offered the classic stature of heroic manliness combined with the fifties image of the lonely long-distance rebel. Both Masterson and Paladin wore black. If Masterson's costume reflected the perverse interior of the outward gentleman, Paladin's definitely branded him a resident west of Eden.

THE MANY LOVES OF DOBIE GILLIS: September 29, 1959–September 18, 1963, CBS.
Executive Producer: George Komack
Producer: Michael Manheim
147 episodes

No other show better exemplified the pre-Beatles Kennedy era than this one. Dobie Gillis (Dwayne Hickman) was a youngster in search of his youth. His wistful flights of fancy were somewhat leveled by the presence of his alter ego, the slovenly Maynard G. Krebs (Bob Denver), all but invisible to the rest of the world, Dobie's personal LBJ.

Each episode brought Dobie, at one point or another, to the statue of "The Thinker," which was inexplicably on loan to and on display in Central City. His weekly ventures into meditation proved to be quite accurate, anticipating the new "Within You Without You" generation of Vietnam eastern-influenced Dobies all across America. Meanwhile, though, back at the high school, Dobie's biology teacher, Mr. Pomfret (William Schallert), was delivering superb lectures to his charges on the futility of love and the fertility of youth, while his potent but vacuous students eagerly awaited the liberation of the bell. These recurring tableaus said more about the educational system in America than all the "Mr. Novacks", "Room 222s" and "Kotters" ever could, Dobie's classroom reflecting the inevitability of the adolescent's rejection of establishment that formal education could never overcome.

Dobie's world was inhabited by beautiful, if unattainable, pubescent teeny boppers, distilled and served up in the gushing guise of Thalia Menninger (Tuesday Weld)—pouty, breasty, lips-teeth-and-tongue oblivious to the desires of Dobie's object. And there was Zelda Gilroy (Sheila James). Zelda seemed even homelier than she was when contrasted with Thalia. The choice here for Dobie was between whimsy and reality, a problem that plagued him everywhere, but just a bit harder sexually.

For Dobie, adulthood and success were inevitable and sterile. He saw his destiny reflected on the face of his father (Frank Faylen) and the facelessness of his mother (Florida Friebus) as they grew old, petty, and bitter, pushing canned foods in a grocery store overly cluttered with an inventory no one seemed particularly interested in buying. Dobie's being constantly harassed by his father to help out in the store seemed like an invitation to his future, something he never quite wanted to participate in.

The series turned an existential corner whenever the camera came in close on Dobie's face, frozen in an unhappy smile, a perverse smirk, his dimples carved in granite rigidity, not unlike that statue. His eyes would darken as he stared beyond the camera, not at it but through it into a terrible dark void, his face revealing what it was meant to cover up. Where did the hippies of the sixties come from? You could do worse than look for early sociological signals from Central City.

THE TWILIGHT ZONE: October 2, 1959–September 18, 1964, CBS.
Executive Producer: Rod Serling
Producers: Buck Houghton, William Froug, Herbert Hirschman
151 episodes (17 one-hour, 134 half-hour)

Intended as fantastic metaphor, these self-consciously derived episodes of "science fiction" came under the auspices of Rod Serling, whose career included apprenticeship in the "golden age" of television drama with at least two remembered, if not memorable, productions ("Patterns" and "Requiem for a Heavyweight"), both of which he wrote.

Based on the continuum of a bad dream, "Twilight Zone" allowed Serling to freely break the rules of character, plot and resolution at the expense of dramatic structure and unity. What appeared to be tales of the unexpected, perhaps in the Hitchcock tradition, were instead terse, illusory skits, blanks in the gun of drama—sounding like discharges, looking like discharges, but missing the gunpowder.

A case in point: Two gamblers, both members of a well-to-do private men's club, are equally annoyed by the attitude and personality of the other. The older of the two challenges the younger to keep silent for one full year. The bet is taken, and the drama begins. Time ticks away. The challenger becomes more desperate and fearful as it becomes obvious he is going to lose. His disgrace is inescapable, for two reasons. First, because he has, indeed, lost. Second, he has strengthened the integrity and the popularity of his opponent. Up to this point there are the makings of good, contemporary drama. Now, though, the "Serling touch." The challenger reveals that he cannot pay off his bet. (Perhaps had we known he was making the bet as a way to win some much needed money, we would have understood the third aspect to his disgrace, as well as the motivation behind his growing desperation. The shift of the drama would have allowed the audience an even greater involvement.)

The opponent, however, has also cheated, having had his vocal cords destroyed, making it impossible for him to speak. So neither one has kept the bet in good faith. There are stylistic attempts to "match" the two men, shooting both in one shot through fish-eye lenses, distorting their visual images to suggest their distorted sense of reality. This is stylistically justifiable (since both men have been shown to be corrupt) but dramatically ambiguous, negating the sense of conflict, equating both men in a distorted vision of dishonesty. In the Serling lexicon, there are neither heroes nor villains, merely people-objects used for demonstration. Without a strong sense of character, the sense of drama is nullified, making conflict and denouement unnecessary. As Serling would put it in his introductions, "The Twilight Zone" was "a fifth dimension, beyond that which is known to man." Serling might have done better if he'd stayed on more familiar ground.

THE UNTOUCHABLES: October 15, 1959–September 10, 1963, ABC.

Executive Producers: Jerry Thorpe, Leonard Freeman
Producers: Howard Hoffman, Alan A. Armer, Alvin Cooperman, Lloyd Richards, Fred Freiberger, Charles Russel, Quinn Martin
114 episodes

"The Untouchables" was a stylistic excursion on the dark side of the street; a perverse, lurid, compelling journey through the manic shadows of the Chicago underworld before, during, and after the Depression. In spite of continual outcries from various civic and ethnic organizations that the show was racist (specifically anti-Italian) and excessively violent, it remained one of the most popular series of its time, commanding a devoted and faithful following. The show came out of the Desilu studio, which, under Desi Arnaz's instruction, spared no expense in re-creating the look and feel of the machine-gun and black-sedan days of the roaring twenties.

Eliot Ness (Robert Stack) was the leader of the Untouchables, a group of automaton federal law enforcers with high ideals in cheap suits. Ness's lack of outward compassion was more than made up for by his seemingly sadistic obsession to wipe out lawlessness in Chicago. The violence of "The Untouchables" seemed justified because, while Ness's men were (by name and by deed) invulnerable, the onus always fell on the criminals. Violence by Ness was in the name of peace—reaction rather than initiative, to restore law and order.

His violence was socially acceptable because it was legally sanctioned. Further, he didn't enjoy his work, a crucial point because his duties weren't merely a job, they were a mission. Criminals dressed better, drank more, lived it up with lots of women, had tons of money and drove fast black cars. This forced Ness and his holy Untouchables to do battle on criminal turf. In the process, Ness became consumed with the criminal world as well as the criminal act. He was forced to dwell underground, creating a situation where right lusted after wrong as much as wrong resisted the temptation to lust after right.

The true conflict in "The Untouchables" was the American moral dialectic between joyless worth and worthless joy.

MY THREE SONS: September 29, 1960–August 24, 1972, ABC/CBS.
Executive Producer: Don Fedderson
Producers: Fred Henry, Edmund Hartmann, George Tibbles
369 episodes

For the most part, family-life situation comedies portray American home life the way it should be rather than the way it is. The family unit becomes largely mythic. There are special exceptions ("Ozzie and Harriet" and "Father Knows Best," for example), but the rule seems to be one of incompleteness; the absence of one or both natural parents, the "norm," creating a situation calling for the remaining members of the family to pull closer together.

Such was the case with the missing-mother family of Don Fedderson's epic family saga "My Three Sons." No delinquents, drug addicts, or social undesirables in the Douglas household, just shoulder-shrugging pipe-smoke wisdom from sage Steven Douglas (Fred MacMurray) elevated to nobility by virtue of raising a family without the benefit of mother in the kitchen and wife in the bedroom. Douglas' redemption came through self-sacrifice, his pleasure through family endurance.

"My Three Sons" was the ultimate sixties family show, lasting through that decade and into the next. In an age when most young men were being confronted with either going to war or working hard at evading the draft, here was a house out of time, not of the sixties at all, reflecting more the collective disposition of the peacetime fifties. Douglas' cardigan complacency suggested Richard Corry ulcers, for his life was one of secrecy. Where did he go when he went to work, or went out of town, as he frequently did? Why did he have an aging male housekeeper when his sons were well into their teens and old enough to cook their own dinner? Why didn't he remarry for all those years, until very late in the series? The implicit homosexual overtones to this show were disturbing and unavoidable.

By the show's end, the mood in America had changed significantly. Fred Silverman decided to replace this situation comedy with another. He removed ''My Three Sons'' to make room for a show Silverman decided to give one last chance in the ratings. A situation comedy that had not done all that well, and was about to get the axe. ''My Three Sons'' was replaced by ''All in the Family,'' and the era of Lear was upon us.

THE ANDY GRIFFITH SHOW: October 3, 1960–September 16, 1968, CBS.

Executive Producers: Sheldon Leonard, Danny Thomas Enterprises

Producers: Aaron Ruben, Richard O. Linke, Bob Ross

249 episodes

THE BEVERLY HILLBILLIES: September 26, 1962–September 7, 1971, CBS.

Executive Producer: Al Simon

Producers: Paul Henning, Joseph DePew, Mark Tuttle

216 episodes

THE FARMER'S DAUGHTER: September 20, 1963–September 2, 1966, ABC.

Producers: Steve Gethers, Peter Kortner, Harry Ackerman

101 episodes

PETTICOAT JUNCTION: September 24, 1963–September 12, 1970, CBS.

Producer: Paul Henning

148 episodes

GILLIGAN'S ISLAND: September 26, 1964–September 4, 1967, CBS.
Executive Producers: William Froug, Sherwood Schwartz
Producers: Jack Arnold, Robert L. Rosen
98 episodes

GREEN ACRES: September 15, 1965–September 7, 1971, CBS.
Executive Producer: Paul Henning
Producer: Jay Sommers
170 episodes

MAYBERRY, R.F.D.: September 23, 1968–September 6, 1971, CBS.
Executive Producers: Andy Griffith, Richard O. Linke
Producer: Bob Ross
78 episodes

One of the more interesting network programing trends began in 1960 and lasted for ten years. Jim Aubrey, then President of the CBS network, was responsible for the "rural revolution" in situation comedies. Deemed advisable by CBS Chairman William Paley as the logical solution to the programing hole developing from the fading Western cycle of the late fifties-early sixties, the idea was to combine the success of the high-riding sitcom cycle with the ruralism of the Westerns; thus was born "corn-pone sitcom," complementing so well the TV down-home humor of Herb Shriner, Red Skelton, and even Jack Benny, all CBS comic icons.

The cycle began with "The Andy Griffith Show." Although ABC tried to follow on the rural trail with "The Farmer's Daughter" and had some mild ratings success, it was a CBS lockup, resulting in that network's ten-year domination of ratings and advertising revenue. The shows had the benefit of wide popular appeal without being overtly controversial; as insular as a Road Runner cartoon (without the socially raised eyebrows at the coyote chasing the Road Runner to do what coyotes presumably love to do most).

"The Andy Griffith Show" gave rednecking a good name with its premise that big cities were really more provincial than small-town U.S.A., that bathtub gin was more patriotic than a New York egg cream. The original pilot of the show had Danny Wilson (Danny Thomas, who produced "The Andy Griffith Show" and allowed his own successful character from "Make Room for Daddy" to appear for the sake of ratings) arrested for speeding and seemingly about to be taken for a ride by wise-guy sheriff Andy Taylor (Andy Griffith). It wasn't until the end of the two-part pilot that we discovered Andy was in fact a swell guy, locking Wilson up his way of defending the rural countryside from the urban invasion by "teaching Danny a lesson": to respect the lives of others by being a little more careful on the road.

Aside from Danny's speeding infraction, there was no crime in Mayberry. Also no Blacks, Jews, Catholics, Puerto Ricans, Chicanos, or young women, presumably what kept Mayberry safe; integration and social responsibilities dangerous urban in-fringements of *Amurrican* individual rights, Andy's apple-pie grin and six-gun symbols of justice, law and order, mom and pop. Andy's job of "raising" the town was personalized by his raising his motherless child, Andy being a traditional TV widower. He depended upon Barney (Don Knotts), his incompetent but honest deputy, for companionship, and on Aunt Bee (Frances Bavier) for apple pie and female supervision for his kid, Opie (Ronny Howard).

If "The Andy Griffith Show" was the first of the rural cycle, the most popular was "The Beverly Hillbillies." The one-joke theme of the "Hillbillies" was that you could take the oil out of the ground, but you couldn't take the crude out of the hillbilly, even when you transplanted him to Beverly Hills. Watching the Clampett clan whoop it up in the rich hills of Los Angeles wasn't the most intense TV experience of the sixties, but given a young buxom blonde (Donna Douglas), an obligatory old woman seniled into fifth childhood (Irene Ryan), and Jed himself (Buddy Ebsen), it wasn't hard to understand why the good ol' folks felt liberated from those city-slicker sitcoms where wives, for some inexplicable reason, called the shots.

"Green Acres" reversed the "Hillbillies" premise, as Oliver

Douglas (Eddie Albert) decided to forsake city life in favor of life on the farm, along with his wife (Eva Gabor) and cow. The joke here was that while living in the city made Douglas constipated, Mrs. Douglas was from Hungary no matter where she hung her mink. Of course it was as impossible for the Douglases to become part of the rural scene as it was for the Hillbillies to gain acceptance in Beverly Hills, the inside smirk that gave the urban TV execs the last condescending laugh.

Displacement was also the theme of "Gilligan's Island," a no-joke affair where the once whimsical Bob Denver, so effective as Maynard in "Dobie Gillis," was wasted as foil for the empty slapstick humor and punch lines delivered by Jim Backus, better off by far as the voice of Magoo.

"The Beverly Hillbillies" lasted eight seasons; "Andy Griffith," eight; "Gilligan's Island," three; "Green Acres," six; "Mayberry, R.F.D.," three; "The Farmer's Daughter," three; "Petticoat Junction," seven. They dominated the network prime-time ratings during the sixties. Yet, by the early seventies they were gone. Every one of them.

COMBAT: October 2, 1962–August 29, 1967, ABC.
Producers: Robert Altman, Gene Levitt, William Self, Selig
          Seligman
152 episodes

THE LIEUTENANT: September 14, 1963–September 5, 1964,
             NBC.
Executive Producer: Gene Roddenberry
Producer: Norman Felton
29 episodes

TWELVE O'CLOCK HIGH: September 18, 1964–January 13,
             1967, ABC.
Executive Producer: Quinn Martin
78 episodes

RAT PATROL: September 12, 1966–September 16, 1968, ABC.
Producers: Mirisch-Rich, Jon Epstein, Mark Weingart
58 episodes

The war/military genre began with "Combat" early in the sixties when a place called Vietnam was all but unknown to the majority of Americans. "Combat," on ABC, was that network's attempt to gain larger audiences by picking up the Western's declining audiences. It was CBS, though, that shrewdly turned toward rural comedy and dominated the ratings for the remainder of the decade.

"Combat," a show that neglected individual characterization emphasis in favor of shrapnel/grenade/bazooka action, had a solid five-year run on ABC, coming to an end when the network replaced the staged action sequences with something better: actual films of the Vietnam War, presented every evening on the network news. In fact, all the peacetime war fantasies faded— "The Rat Patrol," "Twelve O'Clock High" and "The Lieutenant" among the more popular—as the real war in Asia raged on and on.

DR. KILDARE: September 28, 1961–August 30, 1966, NBC.
Producers: David Victor, Calvin Clements, Norman Felton,
**   Herbert Hirschman**
190 episodes (132 one-hour, 58 half-hour)

BEN CASEY: October 2, 1961–March 21, 1966, ABC.
Executive Producers: John E. Pommer, Matthew Rapf
Producers: Wilton Schiller, Jack Laird, James E. Moser
153 episodes

The two dominant medical series of the sixties were "Dr. Kildare" and "Ben Casey"—the former reaching back to the Hollywood forties movie series, the latter to the original "Medic," created and produced by "Casey's" producer, James E. Moser.

The "Kildare" movie series concentrated on the relationship between Dr. Gillespie and "young Dr. Kildare," a love-hate relationship that often pushed Dr. Kildare to heroic heights in the name of love and surgery. Reluctance was heroic in Kildare's movie days, America's entrance into World War II made even more heroic by its seemingly having to be literally shoved by Japan into action.

The attitude was somewhat different when "Kildare" came to television. The professional relationship between Gillespie and Kildare was more father and son, "father" Gillespie (Raymond Massey) offering gentle guidance and assurance with muted respect and admiration for the ambitious, if boyish Dr. Kildare (Richard Chamberlain). TV's Kildare didn't have to be shoved. He in fact did the shoving, arrogance in the name of self-justifying success.

"Ben Casey" (Vince Edwards) was someone else again, a hairy-armed character who seemed to confuse solemnity with dedication, who resented the presence of senile Dr. Zorba (Sam Jaffe) and winced at Zorba's seerlike "Ben Caseeee." If Kildare's Blair Hospital was white-on-white aggression in the name of decency, careerism, and the American Way, Casey's County General Hospital was a smoldering, shadowy world of the perverse, with personnel drama interfering with the general healing process; doctors arguing among themselves, vainly searching for a sense of reason for their endless healing.

Still, the Kildare/Casey era was preoccupied with the holy missions of doctors, overshadowing the real problems of patients. It wasn't until the seventies that TV medicine shifted its focus from the healer to the sick, turning the drama away from endless and inevitable medical denouement toward complex and mortal lines of dramatic conflict.

HOLLYWOOD AND THE STARS: September 30, 1963–September 28, 1964, NBC.
Producers: David L. Wolper, Jack Mulcahy, Jack Haley, Jr.
31 episodes

BRACKEN'S WORLD: September 19, 1969–December 25, 1970,
                  NBC.
Executive Producer: Del Reisman
Producers: George M. Lehr, Stanley Rubin, Robert Lewin
41 episodes

Very few TV programs have dealt directly with the entertainment industry, fewer still with the television industry. There have
been shows whose locale is a TV or a radio station; Mary Tyler
Moore's show, for example, took place in a TV setting, but the
newsroom could just as well have been a fashionable boutique,
with Lou the manager of sales, Ted the floor supervisor, Mary the
bookkeeper. In fact, "The Mary Tyler Moore Show" had very
little to do with television.

"Bracken's World," on the other hand, was a prime-time soap
opera based on Hollywood's only industry: entertainment. Placed
inside the Bracken Studios, the show was concerned with showing what went on behind the scenes, or at least what people like to
think goes on behind the scenes, which is precisely why the show
failed. Gone are the days when people listened to radio drama and
believed the actors were actually acting out their roles rather than
reading them. "Bracken's World" sought to deal with a sophisticated industry, but failed to consider the sophistication of its
viewers.

Another attempt at perpetuating the Hollywood myth rather
than exposing it was "Hollywood and the Stars," a show far
more devious than "Bracken's World" because it assumed the
stature of truth in the form of documentary, utilizing a present-
tense narration, delivered by Joseph Cotten. The overall tone of
veracity did little to lift this series from the level of fan magazine.

Both programs demonstrated the possessive secrecy Hollywood has always sought about itself, apart from its product.
While the official communiques of Hedda Hopper and Louella
Parsons may have seemed like the moral tattletales of Hollywood, they were in fact the levers the studios pulled in order to
keep their stars in line. The only lasting threat to a star under the
studio system was to become box-office poison, and that could
happen if the public was turned off by some scandal, as in the

case of Fatty Arbuckle. Ultimately, the Hollywood industry operates behind closed doors, and the surest way to keep those doors closed is to pretend to open them, to perpetuate the mythic rather than to examine the reality.

THE DICK VAN DYKE SHOW: October 3, 1961–September 7, 1966, CBS.
Executive Producers: Danny Thomas Productions, Sheldon Leonard
158 episodes

A sixties incarnation of "I Love Lucy," "The Dick Van Dyke Show," like its predecessor, utilized show business as a backdrop in which to chronicle the adventures of Rob Petrie (Dick Van Dyke), part of the television writing team that included Buddy (Morey Amsterdam) and Sally (Rose Marie). The action was pretty much split between Rob's work and home life, creating a basic two-set construct, enlarging, but not expanding, the original "Lucy" concept of situation comedy. Once again, show business was nine-to-five suit and tie, while the homesite was more ranchy than raunchy, twin beds still obligatory.

The Petries were sixties mythic: young, successful, conforming, creative, and controlled, convenient party-line (if dated) counterparts to the dope-smoking, acid-dropping radical, sexually liberated flower-power kids of the day. And it's obvious that myth is what the audience preferred, a lack of physical contact was emphasized to ridiculous proportions—Rob kissing Laura (Mary Tyler Moore) as if there were a steel fence between them. Instead of sensual, Laura was "fashionable," while Rob's saving grace was his clumsiness; stumbling and tripping a way of portraying "honest innocence"—God's way of cautioning the helpless (Rob) and flavoring the bland (Laura). Romance was unnecessary after courtship, certainly after the arrival of a child. In order to somewhat vent the Petrie air of any residual cynicism, there was the presence of Buddy and Sally, the sarcastic alternative twosome to the happy household. Buddy and Sally were both unattractive, negative, childless; Buddy unhappily married, Sally unbearably single, both acute representations of the cynical and the ordinary, leading us to accept all the more Rob and Laura in wedded, if unbedded, bliss. To round out the moral continuum, Rob worked for Alan Brady (Carl Reiner), the successful and popular TV host. Brady suffered from megalomania, emergency brake on the vehicle of financial success. In many ways, "The Dick Van Dyke Show" brought the TV sitcom from its crude vitality in the fifties to a studied mythology of the sixties, anticipating a disintegrated social vision for the seventies.

HENNESEY:　September 28, 1959–September 17, 1962, CBS.
Producers:　Jackie Cooper, Don McGuire
96 episodes

McHALE'S NAVY:　October 11, 1962–August 30, 1966, ABC.
Producer:　Edward J. Montagne
138 episodes

THE WACKIEST SHIP IN THE ARMY:　September 19,
　　　　　　　　　　　　　　　1965–September 4, 1966, NBC.
Executive Producer:　Harry Ackerman
Producer:　Herbert Hirschman
29 episodes

MR. ROBERTS:　September 17, 1965–September 2, 1966, NBC.
Executive Producer:　James Komack
30 episodes

HOGAN'S HEROES:　September 17, 1965–July 4, 1971, CBS.
Executive Producer:　Bing Crosby Productions
Producer:　Edward H. Feldman
168 episodes

M*A*S*H: September 17, 1972–still running, CBS.
Executive Producers: Larry Gelbart, Gene Reynolds
Producers: Alan Katz, Don Reo, Burt Metcalfe

The whimsical war shows of the early sixties gave way to the manic battleground absurdities of the post-Vietnam seventies; from the religiosity of "Hennesey" to the sardonic despair of "M*A*S*H," the latter dealing with the American intervention in the Far East years before Hollywood's *Deer Hunter* and *Apocalypse Now* signaled the movie industry's readiness to respond to the major trauma of the times.

Peacetime militarism was seen through the arch cynicism of Sergeant Bilko, followed by the reverence of Lieutenant Hennesey (Jackie Cooper), more saint than sailor, more healer than hunter. The special qualities of the angelic *Mr. Roberts* of stage and screen were reduced on television, twisted to resemble a sitcom marriage between captain and lieutenant. The less said about "McHale's Navy" the better, except to wonder how any of those sailors ever passed a physical. With "Hogan's Heroes" one wonders how a show that made fascism so laughable and lovable could excel in the sixties, while Vanessa Redgrave's prison-camp portrayal of a Jew caught by the Nazis could evoke so much outrage during the more reactionary and "conservative" seventies. The fast and easy answer is that comedy is always taken less seriously than drama, which is why comedy can get away with so much more. However, "Hogan's Heroes" was offensive beyond the obvious, for it implied that there are no prisons, only havens; no villains, only watchguards. The show was an outrageous disgrace and shamed the victims as well as the survivors of the Second World War's special brand of hell.

"M*A*S*H," a program as highly praised as any ever on television, allows liberal and conservative alike to take a breather from the guilt and fear of the Vietnam experience. The cynical Hawkeye (Alan Alda) is a skillful doctor, balancing his bitterness with his ability to operate both on and off the table; the basis for many episodes. His sexual adventures demonstrate how war perverts the sexuality of soldiers, a daring theme, and an interesting perspective for TV to explore.

"M*A*S*H" took other brave steps. The death of Colonel Blake (McLean Stevenson) was handled in a fashion unique to sitcom standards. He died at the end of an episode in which his future appeared anything but fatalistic. True, he died off-screen, and his death was the result of a contract dispute between actor and producer, but nevertheless the remaining members of the unit actually acknowledged Colonel Blake's death unmetaphorically: as death.

On the down side, the elevation of medical corpsmen to "sainthood" was a copout. By having them pull shrapnel out of the wounded they were, in a sense, denying the ravages of war, implying that the situation, like the wound, would simply heal up and go away.

I SPY: September 15, 1965–September 2, 1968, NBC.
Executive Producer: Sheldon Leonard
Producers: Mort Fine, David Friedkin
82 episodes

THE FBI: September 19, 1965–September 8, 1974, ABC.
Executive Producer: Quinn Martin
Producer: Charles Lawton
208 episodes

POLICE WOMAN: September 13, 1974–August 30, 1978, NBC.
Executive Producer: David Gerber
Producer: Douglas Benton
91 episodes

McCLOUD: (NBC Mystery Movie) September 22, 1971–April 17,
                 1977, NBC.
Executive Producer: Glen A. Larson
40 episodes

COLUMBO: (NBC Mystery Movie) September 15, 1971–May 22, 1977, NBC.
Producer: Everett Chambers
40 episodes

STREETS OF SAN FRANCISCO: September 16, 1972–June 23, 1977, ABC.
Executive Producer: Quinn Martin
38 episodes

McMILLAN AND WIFE: (NBC Mystery Movie) September 29, 1971–April 24, 1977, NBC.
Executive Producer: Leonard B. Stern
Producer: Jon Epstein
39 episodes

("COLUMBO," "McMILLAN AND WIFE" AND "McCLOUD" WERE PART OF THE NBC SUNDAY NIGHT MYSTERY MOVIE, WHICH ALSO INCLUDED "AMY PRENTIS," "HEC RAMSEY," "LANIGAN'S RABBI," "McCOY.")

"I Spy" was an official success, highly praised by official approvers for installing Bill Cosby as the first black actor to star in a weekly dramatic network series. Unarguably a right move, if not exactly for the right reasons.

To begin with, Cosby's victory wasn't a "first" at all, but a restoration of Blacks to the network tube after their sheer banishment in the post-"Amos and Andy" era when *no* Blacks was the simplest solution to *which* Blacks, *how* Blacks, and finally *why* Blacks. In an age when the presence of the black actor was enough reason for success, the black character may tend to get overlooked. Scotty (Bill Cosby), part of a government spy team, completed by Kelly Robinson (Robert Culp), was always and forever more virtuous than his partner. Whereas Kelly was ostensibly a free-wheeling tennis pro with an endless stream of willing women, Scotty was his "manager" (read "valet"), not privy to women, wine and songism, preferring to stay up in the hotel room reading Goethe (Scotty was, of course, a Rhodes scholar).

By elevating the moral and intellectual level of one Black, there is the unavoidable suggestion, no matter how oblique, of the elevation of all Blacks. If one accepts the validity of one Black as all in "I Spy," so must one accept it in "Good Times" or "The Jeffersons," shows that preach quite a different sermon. In "Good Times" moral superiority reads as racial passivity, life in the ghetto one long happy joke.

In "The Jeffersons" the anti-White attitude of George Jefferson is an excuse to laugh at his (all Blacks') ignorance, tempered by his white neighbor's being even more obtuse than he is, racial anger one more excuse to laugh hysterically. Finally, all subsequent network Black Characters suffer from being capitalized *at all*, becoming more burlesque than ballet. Therefore, while Scotty in "I Spy" succeeds as a presence (terrifically performed by Bill Cosby), he fails as a character, self-denial an uneasy compromise for being there at all, making "I Spy" a qualified success and a disappointing failure.

After his delirious success with the extraordinary and breathtaking "The Fugitive," Quinn Martin's influence on American dramatic television began to decline. His creative denouement was represented by two subsequent series, "The FBI" and "The Streets of San Francisco." Part of the problem with these shows was their reluctance to acquire a social adaptability for the seventies. The emphasis in "The FBI" and "The Streets of San Francisco" was decidedly male, with femininity a deadly diversion.

Women were gaining in position in the seventies in such shows as "Police Woman," starring Angie Dickinson in the title role. Pepper was sexually aggressive, tempered by moral responsibility allowing for (ahem) undercover work, but only in the name of law and order. Kissing a thief was an occupational hazard for Pepper, never to be confused with real affection. While the relationship between Pepper and Sergeant Crowley (Earl Holliman) was never explicitly unraveled, there were many threads of frustration that made Pepper's official sexual aggression easier to understand.

However, the "appearance" in the seventies of liberated

women more often than not served to take the place of the "spirit" of liberation, resulting in second thoughts about the domestic bang-bang of the pots-and-pans aggression of Edith Bunker and, before her, Alice Kramden, if for no other reason than the familiar sexual link to the kitchen sink is probably easier to identify with for housewives and less threatening than a career police woman's garter belt and hand-cuffs, exposed and closed in the name of law and order. Pepper's thrust was decidedly phallic, her pistol a circumstance of privilege; heady stuff leading to peculiar reactionary trends. "Police Woman" to "Charlie's Angels" becomes a regressive tract, the flaunting of breasts "redeeming" by virtue of the Angels being unattainable.

"Columbo" must be chalked up as a failure because of its poorly coordinated attempt to make clumsiness a virtue, beating the hare/tortoise bit to death. The notion that sloppiness is the style of the preoccupied is an appealing one (as any slob will tell you), especially the married man over forty who made up the bulk of the viewing audience of the little guy in the raincoat. Yet, while Columbo (Peter Falk) was cynically triumphant, his victories were crudely circumstantial, making him seem smarter than he was because those around him, especially the guilty parties, were incredibly dumber. Much dumber. To be expected, since they were all so much neater, wealthier, and better educated.

"McMillan" and "McCloud" were beer-can entertainments—stoic and sophisticated, lacking ironic reasoning, sensitivity, and any apparent skills of detection. McMillan (Rock Hudson) liked to dress in bathrobes whenever possible, making him dependent on his laundry as much as anything else for solving crimes. McCloud (Dennis Weaver) played the sucker-punch gimmick that only cowboys are real men, equally macho with horses or women, able to tell their bosses to get lost, carrying guns and having a hell of a time. McCloud's highest ratings always came out of the East.

In general, the problem with many of the above series was that they lacked any sense of irony in the telling of their stories. A lack of irony leads to a lack of compassion for either victim or predator, resulting in a neutral narrative viewpoint. This turns intensity into whimsy, a crucially inept substitution leaving predictability in its static, wake.

THAT GIRL: September 8, 1966–September 10, 1971, ABC.
Executive Producer: Bill Persky, Sam Denoff
Producers: Bernie Orenstein, Saul Turteltaub, Jerry Davis
136 episodes

Here we have the "plight" of a young girl who, in choosing career over marriage and kids, dares to go out into the big city of New York to "make it." Hailed at the time as a feminist breakthrough for being based on the career pursuit of a single girl, the show nevertheless avoided taking any real chances, its producers satisfied with the illusion of liberation rather than the reality of it.

Ann Marie (Marlo Thomas), surrounded by parental love and money, was engaged to a guy who apparently donated his sex drive to science (Ted Bessell). She managed to cope with the everyday problems of careerism by batting her wide eyes, sighing her husky sighs, and giggling her garbled giggle.

The pursuit of an acting career by a young pretty girl in New York can be a provocative premise for a show. Yet nowhere in "That Girl" was there the slightest hint of casting-couch conflicts (or even a casting couch). Conflict? How long can a girl keep knocking on doors, handle her boyfriend without sex, and reassure her worried parents before she stops smiling? Essentially, "That Girl" dished up the myth of the happy failure, already so prevalent on television, rather than touching upon the sensitive issue of the miserable loser, (let alone the miserable success). Shows such as "That Girl" suggest that all the fun is in the trying, the attempt a sufficient full-time career, especially for women.

STAR TREK: September 8, 1966–September 2, 1969, NBC.
Executive Producer: Gene Roddenberry
Producers: John Meredyth Lucas, Gene L. Coon, Fred
                        Freiberger
79 episodes

A legitimate cult item, "Star Trek" never overcame its poor ratings while a part of the prime-time network schedule, leading to its cancelation at the end of its third year. The fast answer as to why the show never caught on is that it was more hype than hip. A look at how it was scheduled by NBC might provide additional clues.

When "Star Trek" debuted in the fall of 1966 it was scheduled against CBS's long-running, highly successful "My Three Sons," which was followed by a feature movie. ABC offered "The Tammy Grimes Show" followed by the high-rated "Bewitched." Grimes's show bombed, but "Sons" and "Bewitched" continued to thrive in the ratings, both shows siphoning the young audience, a prime target for "Star Trek." Further, "Bewitched" was followed by "That Girl." "That Girl" aired after "Star Trek," but Marlo Thomas' show had strong enough numbers to lift the ratings of "Bewitched."

In its second season, "Star Trek" was up against the final segments of the CBS movie, while ABC eliminated "Tammy Grimes," replacing it with "That Girl." Retaliating, NBC moved "Star Trek" out of its original Thursday evening time slot to the same time (8:30) on Friday. CBS slotted "Gomer Pyle" and the first part of the "CBS Friday Night Movie." ABC all but conceded, throwing "Hondo," an inconsequential Western, at "Star Trek." Even so, "Star Trek" failed to move significantly in the numbers. For the third, and what would prove to be final, season for "Star Trek," NBC moved it further into the night, a crucial mistake. 10:00 EST, 9:00 CST proved to be too late for the Trekkies, also for the post-teen set, out for the night, due back home soon. ABC gained solid numbers with its "Judd for the Defense," a bit of very Mason-like lawyer melodrama for a decidedly mature audience.

As for the show itself, so much has already been made of Spock's ears, the starship *Enterprise*, the Romulans and the Klingons, it seems almost superfluous to take another look. The Trekkies have built a wall of faith around which critical opinion becomes somewhat cynical, praise unnecessary. The plus column shows check marks for the idea of investigating the space of space, for the physical texture of the spaceship *Enterprise*, and for the even-toned study of the chain of command. Captain Kirk's log entries added a stoic, Melvillean touch to the adventures. On the minus side, the unavoidable weakness of William Shatner's performance as Captain Kirk seriously hurt the series. Never as

Spartan as originally conceived, Kirk's inability to dominate a situation went hand in hand with Shatner's inability to dominate a scene, which partially explains the elevation to cult status for the Athenian Mr. Spock (and not Kirk), whose lack of emotion was mistaken at the time for some intergalactic mysticism. As epic, "Star Trek" suffered from a basic lack of character and a resultant lack of good stories. Because action is a result of character, when characters are made to service action, the result is pulp fiction, nothing more, nothing less.

ROWAN AND MARTIN'S LAUGH-IN: January 22, 1968–May 14, 1973, NBC.
Producers: George Schlatter, Paul Keyes

HEE-HAW: June 15, 1969–still running, CBS/syndicated.
Executive Producers: Frank Peppiatt, John Aylesworth
Producer: Sam Lovullo

"Laugh-In" was one of the most popular shows of the late sixties, utilizing a style of disruptive cutting, short blips of scenes, lots of bare skin, and a psychedelic explosion of tits and ass. "Laugh-In" worked because it looked funny. The show reached its impulsive heights when President Nixon guested, saying "Sock it to me" on the air, a prophetic request of monumental proportion.

The show was scatter-shot, stutter-step, montage gone mad—a reflection, all in all, of the psychedelic mood of the day. Eventually, like most sixties fads, this one wound up consuming itself, burning out after a few seasons, taking with it the performing careers of its hosts, Rowan and Martin, neither to be seen again in prime time, relegated to daytime game shows, the Siberia of former network stars.

"Hee-Haw" was CBS's answer to NBC's "Laugh-In." After three network seasons the show was canceled, only to go into perpetual first-run syndication, thriving on the loyalty of rural American TV viewers. The funniest thing on "Hee-Haw" was that bassett hound's wrinkled face, or Roy Clark's when he would astonish himself with his finger-picking abilities on the guitar.

MARCUS WELBY, M.D.: September 23, 1969–May 11, 1976, ABC.
Executive Producer: David Victor
Producer: David J. O'Connell
172 episodes

MEDICAL CENTER: September 24, 1969–September 6, 1976, CBS.
Producer: Frank Glicksman
144 episodes

These two programs complete the cycle of medical series through the first thirty years of network programing. In the seventies the accent was on the patient. These morality tales brought the stories from the factual/medical to the moral/metaphysical, as characters' diseases now seemed to reflect their personalities, illness meted out from above as punishment for moral deficiencies, placing patients in the position of needing deliverance as much as healing. If Dr. Welby (Robert Young) seemed more passive than his predecessors (Styner, Kildare and Casey), it was because he seemed to sense his powers were unlimited. And he was right. His patients usually experienced character-altering revelations just prior to miraculous recoveries, and they were always "better off" for their hospital experience. Marcus' specialty was moral facelifting.

Much the same at the "Medical Center," where doctors once again spent more time trying to figure out why something happened to someone than how to fix it. Hospitals as churches, preachers as doctors, faith healers as faith healers. The one no-no that lasted the entire cycle of medical shows was romantic involvement for the doctors. Even a casual flirtation carried with it highly unfavorable mortality risk for the women. Medical doctors/

missionaries had to abstain from all temptation in order to properly heal the metaphysically ill, whose symptoms seemed to respond to the most mysterious of all medicines, moral rectitude.

Finally, if audiences identified with the patients in the seventies more than with the doctors, it was because seeking salvation and receiving forgiveness was more comforting than selfless sacrifice. Complacency over assertion, TV's favorite theme told here in different, if familiar, stories.

THE MARY TYLER MOORE SHOW: September 19, 1970–September 3, 1977, CBS.
Executive Producers: James L. Brooks, Allan Burns
Producers: Stan Daniels, Ed Weinberger
168 episodes

RHODA: September 9, 1974–December 9, 1978, CBS.
Executive Producers: James L. Brooks, Allan Burns
Producers: Charlotte Brown, David Davis, Lorenzo Music
96 episodes

PHYLLIS: September 8, 1975–August 30, 1977, CBS.
Executive Producers: Ed Weinberger, Stan Daniels
48 episodes

Mary Richards (Mary Tyler Moore) seemed very much the seventies version of the sixties' Laura Petrie (Mary Tyler Moore), so much so that one might see them as literally the same character: Mary (Laura), divorced from Rob and freed from the pleasant imprisonment of the sixties suburbia syndrome, comes to the big city to find her own identity in the very field where her husband excelled—television. So it was we found her, in the first episode, landing a job in a television newsroom working for TV news producer Lou Grant (Ed Asner), never speaking of her past, looking only to "make it on her own."

It soon became clear that Mary didn't have a job at all but was on some kind of divine maternal mission. The tensions in the newsroom rarely involved a late-breaking story, reflecting instead the personal conflicts among the "team."

There was gruff, 'neath-it-all-heart-of-gold-leaf-lettering Lou, to whom Mary was a hand-holding, den-mothering, drinking buddy and repressed sex object; Ted Baxter (Ted Knight), to whom she was the deflating, den-mothering, repressed sex object; and Murray (Gavin MacLeod), to whom she was the den-mothering repressed male sex object. Any "me"-decade liberationist stirrings Mary may have experienced seem now inconsequential, smothered by her own lack of political smarts and the overall suppression of her ego by fat, unhappy Lou. Elevation to single-girl careerist brought along with it the burden of being nice to the boss, in the sexist male power structure of office politics. Desexualized for the TV audience, Mary was more mom to Lou than lover. Lou, prevented from obligatory ass-grabbing by virtue of his engulfing depression, brought on by his envy of and hatred for the better-looking Ted Baxter and the more talented Murray, was caught between being mothered by Mary and playing big brother protecting the vulnerable, sensitive Murray from the boorish Ted (while preserving Ted's facade in the name of ratings). Mary, at least, gave partial venting to Lou's sexually debilitating depressions by providing the illusion of a nonsexual flirtation.

If one half of Mary's life was involved with the boys in the newsroom, the other half was taken up with the business of domesticity. If Mary was too threatening for the other women at work, especially Sue Ann (Betty White), the lusty, happy homemaker who knew how to keep the home happier than anybody else on the show, she was just what the doctor ordered for the girls back at the apartment complex. This bunch were all losers; Rhoda (Valerie Harper) for instance, destined to spin off into her own Monday night series, a tough enough night of the week to watch television; the start of another work-night stretch after a weekend of disco and disappointments.

Rhoda was appropriately fat, unhappy and neurotic (TV code words for single, New York and Jewish), the perfect commiserator for the Monday-night blues. The series failed when Rhoda presumably found happiness married to a tall, good-looking, sand-brained redneck with a speech defect, and was unable to be saved even by a hopefully depressing, possibly suicidal divorce.

Another neighbor who spun off into Monday night and oblivion was Phyllis (Cloris Leachman). In perpetual change-of-life, her self-hatred was aired through a sexless marriage providing Phyllis with a substantial lack of self-esteem which helped to turn every minor incident into Elizabethan tragedy. And of course there was Georgette (Georgia Engel), a dumb blonde type who was sexually voracious and destined to marry and fall in love with Ted Baxter, a fate worse than life.

"The Mary Tyler Moore Show" was hailed as a fresh approach to the portrayal of women on television. It was a revelation that Mary Richards could sleep around even if she wasn't in love. Leaving moral issues aside, it wasn't that great a coup. If Mary's over-thirty-and-divorced angst gave her round heels, it also allowed her to effectively sidestep her own problems with intimacy. Poor Mary. Always a bridesmaid. Someone should have told her it's better to live with "honeymoon bladder" than to die trying to get it.

JULIA: September 17, 1968–May 25, 1971, NBC.
Producer: Hal Kanter
86 episodes

SANFORD AND SON: January 14, 1972–September 2, 1977,
**   NBC.**
Producers: Bernie Orenstein, Saul Turteltaub
Executive Producers: Norman Lear, Bud Yorkin
136 episodes

GOOD TIMES: February 1, 1974–August 1, 1979, CBS.
Executive Producers: Norman Lear, Allan Manings
Producers: George Sunga, Bernie West, Don Nicholl, Austin and
**   Irma Kalish**
120 episodes

THE JEFFERSONS: **January 18, 1975–still running, CBS.**
Executive Producers: Norman Lear, George Sunga
Producer: Jack Shea

As the black community began to acquire greater purchasing power toward the end of the sixties, TV advertisers, along with producers and networks, began to direct their attentions and their investments accordingly. Thus began the black sitcom cycle of the seventies, beginning with "Julia," a show noted here for its black star, all-white supporting cast and all-white community environment. The schemata was 1960s liberal: mix white with black and you get gray, darkening the white and lightening the black, all for the better. The official party line hailed "Julia" as a "breakthrough," while privately frowning over the lack of any great audience following for the show. In fact, "Julia's" ratings were low enough to suggest that if the show didn't have official status as a socially "progressive" document, it might have been canceled after a few episodes. NBC was reluctant to do so, probably out of fear of racist accusation, an attack in the early seventies that could bring severe economic penalties. NBC kept the show on the air, low ratings and all, for three full TV seasons— not quite enough to make it prime syndication material (the magic number four seasons), but enough to gain respect for the commitment. Julia (Diahann Carroll) was a career nurse, an unfortunate choice, nursing being a classically subservient role. Further, she was a widow with a young son, standard sitcom cliché structure providing a family without the bother of a husband, eliminating sexual tension. Julia worked for a white doctor, continuing the give-and-take of "permissive" racial balance disguised as courageous racial progress. The very fact that the show gained so much attention for its "progressive" stance made its episodes self-conscious and unyielding, a failed if well-intentioned effort.

Still, it began a cycle that included "Sanford and Son," "Good Times," and "The Jeffersons." Few shows in the seventies were as successful in the ratings as "Sanford and Son," which spawned two sequels: "Sanford Arms" and "Sanford." Sanford (Redd Foxx), a junkman, was the personification of Norman Lear's excursion into the black ethos. There was very little white under the collar in this series, the only noticeable concession being the necessary sanitizing of the Redd Foxx X-rated nightclub persona which had previously kept him off the tube for most of his career. There isn't much more to say about this series except that it was a prime showcase for the bizarre talents of Foxx. If the show was funny, it was because Foxx is funny. If it was pedantic, it was because Lear is pedantic. Sanford was no Archie Bunker, and for that there are thanks and regrets. Perhaps a black Archie might have been more "significant," a leap forward, even if a bit of pride might have been lost in the wash.

"Good Times," still another Lear product, lacked charm, wit, sophistication, and the rhythm of inner-city life, here falsified and politicized in the name of situation comedy. Nothing seems more false than watching a ghetto family enjoying poverty, reveling in one-liner happiness while living in a stone-cold apartment, in a bleak city-owned project. Nowhere in "Good Times" was there any attempt to portray the anger and bitterness which, rather than keeping families together, often tears them apart. When the father (John Amos) left the family (and the show because of contractual negotiation), his "desertion" was glossed over; it could have been death or desperation or disgust. Whatever, the effect on his family was so positive it suggested he should have left a lot sooner. Of course, social reality is not a prerequisite for situation comedy any more than is an obligation to be realistic. However, when a social milieu is referred to as part of the basic construct of a show, such as the poverty and project *mise-en-scene* of "Good Times," it must be considered part of the goods. The social pinprick is Norman Lear's stock in trade..

With "The Jeffersons," there is still more Lear-ing. George Jefferson (Sherman Hemsley) just doesn't like white folks, and that's it. This bloody premise has potential for social investigation as well as truly funny situations. Unfortunately, the potential is squandered by particularly sub-Learian writing, the episodes filled with character-change resolution and constant one-lining with the frequency of a bad tic, reducing the show to boredom and ennui. It's just not enough for a show to rely upon race or sex without placing its characters in provocative situations in order to create a context able to withstand weekly renewal and revitalization.

Finally, for Lear, his time may have passed, even as he managed to pass the status quo a decade ago with the landmark "All in the Family." We now know what's happening, baby; what else is new?

ALL IN THE FAMILY (ARCHIE BUNKER'S PLACE):
January 12, 1971–still running, CBS.
Executive Producer: Norman Lear

Once sitcom stylistics were set, late in the fifties, few innovations were attempted. Success meant economic reward, which in turn meant taking no chances. The stylistic standard included the dominant use of the medium shot, the rhythmic cutting of shots on the dialogue line so that when a character spoke the camera was on him, or her, in a one-shot, and then returned to a matching one-shot for the reply, and so on. Close-ups were used as little as possible, since the implicit intensity was a visual not comically applicable. Emphasis was on the objectivity that came with the medium shot and the occasional long, objective fourth-wall shot for a physical bit of business that needed *mise-en-scene* documentation.

Norman Lear was the first to challenge sitcom stylistics by revising the basic inventory of acceptable camera shots, which in turn introduced aspects of drama into comedy, bringing "All in the Family" perhaps closer to the complex urban problems of the working class than was previously thought feasible. The close-up had been used before in situation comedy, notably in "The Many Loves of Dobie Gillis." However, it was Lear's use of that shot against an elongated background that included the diminished image of Edith (Jean Stapleton) which gave an added sense of distance behind the close-up face of Archie Bunker (Carroll O'Connor); a tableau emphasizing isolation, frustration and receding intimacy. It's important to distinguish innovation from invention. Lear is not being credited here with inventing camera angles or as the first to visualize emotional contexts but rather as the first to have coordinated a "new" stylistic overview, giving a new "look" to, as well as taking a fresh look at, situation comedy.

In the beginning Archie was humorless, neofascist, antisemitic, anti-black, anti-everything—a Klanner in search of a white sale. He supported Nixon before and after Watergate, and disliked Carter before and after his election. He hated what his son-in-law stood for politically, and what he did to his daughter, personally (he married her). Over the years, though, things did change. Archie began to deal openly with his affection for "the meathead" (Rob Reiner) as his (Archie's) desperate desire for family unity outweighed political, social, and even racist feelings. He even felt bad when his black neighbor moved away, suggesting that Archie's was the face of the vulnerable liberal beneath the mask of the paranoid conservative. This view (pick away the scab of a conservative and you have the blood of a liberal) put Lear and his program on a precarious critical fence. For the liberals, Lear didn't go far enough with Archie's "education," while for the conservatives Archie's closet liberalism made him an object of ridicule rather than affection, whose ineffective posture symbolized his political softness. Lear was attacked for being nothing more than antisemantic, patted on the head for the nice try, smacked on the bottom for not drawing the dramatic lines clearly or strongly enough. Perhaps overlooked was the fact that Archie Bunker was the first head-of-a-household in a sitcom who, right or wrong, angelic or tainted, was the you-better-have-the-dinner-on-the-table-or-else blue-collar New Yorker who didn't gave a shit about anything, and didn't take shit from anybody. Lear turned this trick by making Archie a slob, but a lovable one, while in total command of his home—"lovableness" presumably softening his ignorant domination of his wife, daughter and son-in-law, allowing both left and right to laugh at, rather than with, Archie. No one had to go into the bathroom with Archie to hear the toilet flush, but everyone was certainly relieved to laugh.

Further, Lear allowed his characters to go beyond the sitcom status quo in a number of interesting ways. Michael, for all his heroic defense of the political left was a potbellied, lazy, loud, overfed armchair activist, while Gloria (Sally Struthers), his wife and Archie's daughter, combined Edith's humor with Archie's obstinance, the result felt most strongly by Michael, whom she effectively tamed from a state of implied outrage to one of demonstrative petulance. It was as if the Archie-Edith personality ratio were inverted to allow us to see the other side of the Bunker power axis, so that Sally became a "what if?" female Archie, with Michael an educated (but not intelligent) Edith.

To its critics, "All in the Family" too closely resembled "The Honeymooners." Not true. While there was a certain working-class similarity between the Brooklyn of the Kramdens and the Queens of the Bunkers, Ralph was the inner-city civil servant whose household was devoid of children, a crucial factor determining the bickering and childlike tantrums Ralph (and Alice) indulged in; whereas the Bunkers were products of the tired suburban middle-class, veterans of the World War Two generation who bought the whole package—twenty-year GI mortgage on the home in the suburbs, beautiful child, three squares a day. So where did it all go wrong? In a place where Ralph Kramden would never have a chance to find out. For Bunker was the cynic who realized it all wasn't what it was cracked up to be, while Kramden remained the beggar seeking a chance to find out what it wasn't like in the first place.

MAUDE: September 12, 1972–April 29, 1978, CBS.
Executive Producers: Norman Lear, Rod Parker
Producers: Bob Weiskopf, Bob Schiller
142 episodes

Lear took his psycho-suburban examination of America a step further with "Maude" (Bea Arthur), Archie Bunker's alter ego. Maude first appeared in an "All in the Family" episode before being spun off into a series of her own. Female, liberal, well-educated, she too had the underbelly of her social posture exposed to reveal her feminism as an extreme reaction to her four passive husbands. Her liberalism cloaked her fear of being at heart, a sexist. Her education was official affirmation of her street-smart sense but also revealed a fear of being not smart enough.

Her house, husband and daughter were like the heart, brains and courage the Lion, Scarecrow and Tin Man. They were there all the time; that wasn't the problem. The fear that they weren't, that was. To dramatize Maude's personality, Lear cast her as a loud, boisterous, selfish, petulant, melodramatic pain in the ass with the saving grace of a razor-sharp wit that cut across the pathos of a woman losing her youth and looks, receding into middle-aged bitterness and moral cellulite. As was the case with Archie, the home was a household populated with relations; a comfortable dwelling in a gilded cage. In Maude's case the American dream was less a case of unfulfillment or disillusionment than a nightmare of fulfillment and illusion—keeping up with the Joneses for the sake of the Joneses. Maude's frustrations weren't as political or rigidly class-structured as Archie's, but more sexual in nature. Rooted in monogamy, money and marriage, Maude saw her plight as male-induced. Her agressiveness and feminist activism were easy to take—failed attempts at any liberation in a society (and industry) that fears change.

The final episode of the series moved Maude to Washington, to Congress, and to the limit, for a successful Maude Findlay presented a whole new set of circumstances that, for better or worse, were never dealt with during the run of the show. With "Maude," as with all of Norman Lear's shows, the results were qualified. If the shows weren't "funny," it's because they focused on problems nontraditionally: long lenses depicted distorted relationships; alcohol repressed frustration; shouting covered up the silence. Maude and Walter's excessive laughing only served to emphasize the lack of humor in their lives.

THE BOB NEWHART SHOW: September 16, 1972–September 2, 1978, CBS.
Executive Producers: Jay Tarses, Tom Patchett, Michael Zinberg
142 episodes

"The Bob Newhart Show" represented the "less is more" theory of situation comedy. Newhart's lack of a distinctive characterization made Dr. Hartley lovable; the show's lack of psychological or even comedic insight made it popular; the lack of supporting-player development made them all endearing. Dr. Hartley's world was sterile and unfulfilled, redeemed only partially by the presence of his hot if frustrated wife, Emily (Suzanne Pleshette), whose wry sarcasm fed on Hartley's passive passion and compensated for the implicit lack of sexual relations between them.

A case can be made for the stylistic slow-take determination of Newhart's brand of sitcom comedy, indirectly derived from Harry Langdon's silent-movie humor. The similarities are many: deliberate pacing, reticent reaction, implied fragility. The difference is a glaring one, and it falls squarely on Newhart's shoulders. The lack of despair in Dr. Hartley signals a lack of self-awareness. While the presence of despair made Langdon's humor poignant, its absence left Newhart's pointless; one-liners became relentless, their repetition underscored by the laughtrack.

It seems as if the normal reaction to everything in situation comedy is a burst of laughter, the absence of that burst a terrifying suspension of a daily reality of life, leading eventually to the suspension of life itself. Laughter then becomes mandatory, humor no longer a prerequisite, jokes no longer funny. With "The Bob Newhart Show" the abundance of laughter and the lack of apparent conflict reflected more hysteria than humor, leaving only those viewers still with their wits about them having any cause for alarm.

THE ODD COUPLE: September 24, 1970–July 4, 1975, ABC.
Executive Producers: **Garry Marshall, Jerry Belson, Harvey Miller, Sheldon Keller**
Producer: Tony Marshall
114 episodes

This representative property of Neil Simon demonstrated nothing so much as his inability to write about male-female relationships. His earlier work either avoids the subject totally, or deals with it obliquely, as in the case with "The Odd Couple." According to Simon, any woman over twenty who is accessible is also overweight, house-robed, Jewish, and chronically addicted to hair curlers. His attempts at sexual confrontation are ludicrous. In his later works, including "Chapter Two," the barriers between intimate relationships are more interesting, more the stuff of drama, if not intimacy. Typically, with Simon, husbands are workhorses who prefer the card table to the bed, especially when the bed is filled with a lump of cold cream masquerading as a wife. At least at the card table, the choice of whether or not to ante is still a male decision.

If "The Odd Couple" fails as situation comedy, it's because of a lack of development beyond the single joke—e.g., the slob and the neat freak sharing an apartment. Here is a situation were TV's structured requirement for repetition ruined the delicate balance the original play had.

The two main characters, Oscar (Jack Klugman) and Felix (Tony Randall), were stale, middle-aged and washed out, not very interesting to deal with, made even less so by the clichéd performances of Randall and Klugman, both of whom reacted to every situation of every episode predictably and boringly, a case of gesture and mannerism substituting for characterization and performance.

KOJAK: October 24, 1973–April 15, 1978, CBS.
Executive Producer: Matthew Rapf
Producers: James MacAdams, Jack Laird
118 episodes

STARSKY AND HUTCH: September 10, 1975–August 21, 1979, ABC.
Executive Producers: Aaron Spelling, Leonard Goldberg
Producer: Joseph T. Naar
92 episodes

Nothing in this series—not the two cardboard heroes whose macho heroics approached the ceremonially insane, not the villains, castrated misunderstood types who were never very good-looking, not the hookers with hearts, the pimps with souls, the good-guy cops or the bad-guy pushers—was quite so carefully developed as the car Starsky and Hutch (Paul Michael Glaser and David Soul) used. Burning rubber was the extent of dramatic friction, the withholding of male tenderness an adolescent depiction of male stoicism.

Starsky and Hutch were L.A. cops, West Coast versions of

New York's street-tough Kojak, shrewdly played by Telly Savalas, whose own definition of "macho" was smug superiority. In true New York tradition, Kojak never left the "house" unless he had to. And when that happened, it wasn't a noble mission, it was a pain in the ass. He worked a job, macho dues-paying style. Kojak's middle-aged cynical today was Starsky and Hutch's inescapable tomorrow.

CHICO AND THE MAN: September 13, 1974–July 21, 1978, NBC.
Executive Producer: James Komack
Producers: Hal Kanter, Michael Morris, Alan Sacks
88 episodes

By the early seventies, racism was no longer a "problem," judging by American television. Ethnicity was, in fact, a great source of humor, insight, wisdom, and bucks. Oh, there were still a few craggly old folks who hadn't heard the news. Folks like Ed Brown (Jack Albertson), whose only real problem was lack of exposure; his racism a by-product of old age, acceptable because of its being so easily correctible. The solution: have Chico (Freddie Prinze) hang around the garage for a while.

The problems with the show were obvious. First, Ed couldn't "change"; that would end the premise of the series and take whatever passed for conflict out of the plots of the episodes. Second, Chico was such a good kid that Spiro Agnew would have had little trouble accepting him. The scripts implied that Chico was tough, street-delinquent, unrepentant, malicious, capable of violence. He may have had a street-tough veneer, but underneath he was all love, gosh and gee-whiz. How much more interesting if, when some of that veneer had been rubbed away by Ed's engine cloth, a blasting rage had been exposed. But that would have been a show of a different color.

Further, Ed was so thoroughly unlikable he managed to give old age a bad name. His role was actually one of straight man to Prinze, who'd begun his career on the nightclub floor, as did James Komack, who made a habit of taking second-rate stand-ups and putting them in second-rate sitcoms, like Prinze in

"Chico" and Gabe Kaplan in "Welcome Back, Kotter," another of Komack's attempts to "look good" as long as one didn't look close.

WELCOME BACK, KOTTER: September 9, 1975–August 3, 1979, ABC.
Executive Producer: James Komack
Producers: Eric Cohen, Alan Sacks
98 episodes

The nightclub syntheses of Kaplan/Kotter, Kaplan/Komack, and ultimately Kotter/Komack form the point of view for this sterile and false attempt to look into the lives of the students and teachers of a remedial Brooklyn high-school class. There wasn't a moment of truth in this entire series—not in the sense of triumph felt by Kotter (Gabe Kaplan) when he returned to the classroom he came out of to inspire others to achieve the heights he'd attained; not in the compassion felt by Kotter with his charges as he identified with their position and tried to uplift them; not in the attitudes of his "gang" of kids toward each other, the most fey and passive group of rebels ever to have had the nerve to show up in a tough Brooklyn school without expecting to get their heads busted by that sadistic breed that preys on the helpless in the hallways.

The series opted for the easy laugh, with Kaplan taking every opportunity to practice his nasal, boring line readings while his students demonstrated their remedial personalities: Vinnie Barbarino (John Travolta), restricted from displaying the true conceit of the working-class, Italian anti-intellectual he so accurately captured in *Saturday Night Fever;* Juan (Robert Hegyes), a Puerto Rican quite removed from the street-hit New York P.R. life; Freddie "Boom-Boom" Washington (Lawrence Hilton-Jacobs), a Black with no street smarts and no hostile chip toward the oppressive hand he'd been dealt; and Arnold Horshack (Ron Palillo), played especially offensively as a gay Jewish weakling, a caricature so frightening that Palillo worked against being identified with it in every other role he played away from the show, much to the great disinterest of audiences everywhere.

Kotter's adventures were without meaning. The closest the series came to the dead-end school life of its students was when Travolta "dropped out of school" (the show) to make it in the movies. Once Travolta left, the TV audience dwindled fast. It seemed that, after all, no one was really interested in a show that celebrated individual weakness rather than triumph over one's limitations.

LAVERNE AND SHIRLEY: **January 27, 1976–still running, ABC.**
Executive Producers: Garry Marshall, Thomas L. Miller, Edward K. Milkis
Producers: Mark Rothman, Lowell Ganz, Monica Johnson, Eric Cohen, Tony Marshall, Thomas L. Milkis

No more a series about the fifties than "Happy Days," "Laverne and Shirley" sold revisionism in the name of one-liners. The time span of "Laverne and Shirley" is actually the early sixties, after Eisenhower and before The Beatles. The background is the Kennedy Era, the foreground the closet in which two repressed lesbians—Laverne (Penny Marshall) and Shirley (Cindy Williams)—prefer each other's, uh, company over that of their parents, boyfriends, and other girlfriends. This makes for terrific sitcom material—a TV-coded marriage without explicit sexual complications. When Laverne pins Shirley to the sofa, hands over head, legs spread by knees, in order to "convince" her about something or other, all is well and good on the obvious plot level, all is well and perhaps even better in the shady area of sexuality, with Laverne, the man, doing the pinning, and Shirley, the woman, not seeming to notice she's being pinned. Or not seeming to mind.

Taking the unusually sophisticated premise of two latent lesbians living in pre-coming-out days, the show suppressed its own boldness by turning revisionist, and presenting a strange years-ago parental philosophy on the whole affair: parents forgive all; the closet will eventually turn into a spare bedroom; whatever skeletons are in one's closets can't really hurt all that much. It seems that by not taking any position on the provocative combination offered, the effect is to normalize the obvious, neuter the extremes, while adding fire to the implications.

On another level, the Marshall plan is quite evident in "Laverne and Shirley." The physical movement is minimal, the blocking stagey and restricted, serving only to accentuate the overrated physicality of Penny Marshall's one-of-the-boys image. The point is made weekly that the show is filmed "before a live audience." Rather than giving us the feeling that we are watching something "live," we are in fact reminded of the distance between us and the performance. The soundtrack filled with hysterical laughter reminds us that the event is historical, having been recorded sometime in the past.

And a final word about those laugh-tracks. Most shows, even those with live audiences, augment audience reactions with laugh-track machines using old tapes from radio for their source of howls. For the most part, the people we hear laughing so hysterically have been dead for many years.

THREE

From the Inside

The following is taken from a series of interviews I conducted with a prominent television writer. Her responses have been edited, although everything included is verbatim.

A television series begins with an idea. A professional TV writer or producer meets with network people to discuss a program idea. The idea will be pitched to the head of development of the network. Without a network, no one can develop a series for prime-time viewing.

An idea is usually given to the networks in planned order. Today a comedy series should not go to NBC first, because they are not strong in that area. A writer is paid several thousand dollars by a production company to do an initial outline. The production company receives no payment from the network to develop the outline, hoping they will receive a go-ahead on the first draft, eventually getting to the pilot script stage. At this point the network will pay up to fifty thousand dollars to the writer, while the production company still receives nothing and won't until the pilot is sold to the network.

It takes a tremendous amount of time to develop and sell a show. A season, maybe two, will go by before a company will make a penny from a script. This is one of the reasons why new production companies are usually formed by people from other successful production companies. The savy is there, the financial planning realistic.

Realistically, it's in the network's interest to keep the bigger production companies in business. Each network might buy one or two pilots from them every season, which helps keep the production company's doors open. The networks try to spread the business around to prevent any one production company from becoming too powerful.

What happens during the development stage for a TV show at a typical pilot script meeting? Someone will say, "That's a wonderful character. A newscaster going after a story. Now let's build in all the elements that will make it work. Let's give him a home base, which is his office. Maybe his home also." Mary Tyler Moore introduced that, and for a while all the new series tried half-home, half-office formats. "The home is easy. Let's give him a landlady and a neighbor. The office has a secretary, preferably dumb, incompetent and funny. She's female of course, unless you want to switch and make her a man. Let's give him a 'helper' who's dumb and keeps getting him into trouble, a boss who's gruff with a heart of gold, somebody below him to push around. Some love interest, a pal to talk to maybe." At the end of the meeting you have every potential circumstance worked out week by week. One week the plot may be one problem, the next week another, but essentially it's always the same. The people who watch aren't disappointed. They're going to see their favorites do their thing the same way as the week before and the week before that. And the series before that. The reason they keep tuning in is because there's a cute girl playing the secretary and a nice old character actor for the boss. TV situation comedy is relationships, not stories. Which is why the producers of "The Paper Chase" probably felt they had a winner. In spite of the intelligent buildup and "Waltons" hype in terms of the show's "value," there was a hero who was lovable and righteous, there was a "boss" who was "gruff" but with a heart of gold. What's different there? They may have tried to attack it from a slightly different angle, but you could tune in that show every week and watch the hero get into conflict with his gruff boss who really loved him. The hero would do the right thing in the end and maybe learn some lesson but never question anything. It was probably a cut above the regular series, but it certainly didn't break any new ground. There was that home base, the classroom, and the law professor's office, and the law professor's secretary.

And the friends of the hero who were all subservient to him, and comical in their own little way.

The producer's concern was the audience watching week after week. TV producers don't want audiences looking in *TV Guide* to see what that week's episode is about. They want to keep the audience hooked, steady customers. Philosophically, producers believe if you aim for mediocrity, you'll probably get something not too far from mediocre. If you aim for greatness, you risk being terrible, not smart for TV. Greatness isn't rewarded on TV, even if you achieve it. The industry feeling, beyond the press clippings, is that the greatest, most progressive episode of any series will still be seen by exactly the same number of people who saw the show the week before, and probably the same as the week after. To most producers, it isn't worth taking chances.

When a show gets a go-ahead to pilot, the search for a cast begins (unless the show is a vehicle for a star). Endless meetings take place to make sure the script is inoffensive, pleasing to all concerned, and if it's a comedy, funny. The goal is a very, very safe pilot. The pilot is tested at various "preview" screenings.

Producers and networks want to make sure the preview audience's reaction is typical. They want the normal, average American audience. In Los Angeles it all boils down to how a typical preview audience, at a special screening house in Los Angeles reacts to a Mr. Magoo cartoon. The "Magoo" has a pretested level of expected laugh reactions. If the preview audience fails to meet that level, the evening is a total waste. It doesn't matter how much the audience likes the shows, or hates the shows; no statistics are taken. The results are discarded and they start over again another night. There's a certain point in the cartoon when Mr. Magoo falls off a mountain that has more to do with what America watches on television than anything else.

Producers lose money every time an episode of their series is broadcast on the network. Networks have complete quality control, and their demands can cause a half-hour episode's budget to balloon way over a hundred thousand dollars, depending upon whether the show is being shot on three-camera tape, three-camera film, or the most expensive way, one-camera film. Film is more expensive to use than tape. Three-camera tape or film is used when a show is shot "live," with simultaneous recording of the action from several angles. One-camera film means that each scene is set up individually and shot, not necessarily in sequence.

The network pays a licensing fee to the production company, per episode, these days anywhere from two hundred seventy thousand to six hundred thousand dollars. Usually, if the show is a success, the licensing fee will be raised after the first year, but nowhere in line with what happens with the demands of the "stars" of the shows, which are met by producers wanting to keep the original "chemistry" of the actors intact. If "X" production company is producing a successful series, or even at the pilot stage if it has a show that the networks think is going to be a winner, but the producers have run out of money, the studio where the show is being produced sometimes makes up the financial difference, for a piece of the show. It then becomes a situation of "X" productions in association with "Y" studios.

Producers make their money in syndication. After the initial plays of a show under the network licensing-fee arrangement, the ownership of a show reverts to the production company. The sale of series—*strips*, as they are called—to syndication, daytime or nighttime, usually for daily viewing, is almost pure profit. Since the network has the final say as to whether a series is canceled during its initial run, the network has the real control of the airwaves. It is in the producer's interests to work as closely and as congenially with the networks, for the reward of a series hit. The fee for a syndication rerun of a hit series may run several thousand dollars. Occasionally, not often, the figure may hit upwards of thirty-five, forty thousand dollars for three or four runs. The details are handled by a syndication that leases the episodes to individual stations, making its own deals and returning a set figure to the original producer.

A production company will lose money if a show runs for two years on the network and is then canceled. Rarely will you see a show that's had that limited a run get into syndication, regardless of its intrinsic artistic or entertainment value, simply because there aren't enough episodes to run on a daily basis. Usually a show has to run a good four years before it goes into syndication. On the other hand, when you see a show in syndication while the series is still on the network, it's usually a tip-off that the production company is in need of money and cashing in early to offset the financial crunch. Paradoxically, the more popular a production outfit becomes—say, six or seven shows in prime time—the faster it's losing money.

Finally, there is no "artistic" community in television to stand up for a show's "quality." You have the original writer and/or creator of a pilot, who may or may not be there beyond the first script. Writers have the least to do with the rest of the corporate/financial/producing end of TV shows. The ideal concept is assembly-line production. In that circumstance, everyone is easily replaceable behind the camera and often in front. If a writer wants to work in television he begins his career with the attitude of compromise, and he never loses it. The "artistic" content of a show doesn't matter to anybody in production. Actors fight for their own moments on camera, trying to make sure they're getting enough exposure, enough punch lines, tube time, etc. Even when they become stars they don't become the moral/artistic guidelines for their shows. And if they aren't stars, they are completely expendable. Most every one in television is happy if he simply doesn't come off looking foolish.

FOUR

The Fall Network Schedules—1946–80.

The noted times are Eastern Standard/Daylight time.

SUNDAY 1946

	7:00	7:30	8:00	8:30	9:00	9:30	10:00	10:30
DUMONT			[......... Western Movie ....]					
CBS								
NBC			Face to Face	Television Screen Magazine				
			Geographically Speaking					
ABC								

MONDAY 1946

	7:00	7:30	8:00	8:30	9:00	9:30	10:00	10:30
DUMONT								
CBS								
NBC		Esso Newsreel	Voice of Firestone					
			Televues					
ABC					[... Gillette Cavalcade of Sports ...]			

TUESDAY 1946

	7:00	7:30	8:00	8:30	9:00	9:30	10:00	10:30
DUMONT			Play the Game		Serving Through Science			
CBS								
NBC								
ABC								

WEDNESDAY 1946

	7:00	7:30	8:00	8:30	9:00	9:30	10:00	10:30
DUMONT				Faraway Hill				
CBS								
NBC								
ABC								

THURSDAY
1946

	7:00	7:30	8:00	8:30	9:00	9:30	10:00	10:30
DUMONT					Cash and Carry			
CBS								
NBC		Esso Newsreel	[.... Hourglass ....]					
ABC					Fight Film Filler			

FRIDAY
1946

	7:00	7:30	8:00	8:30	9:00	9:30	10:00	10:30
DUMONT								
CBS								
NBC			You Are an Artist / Let's Rhumba / I Love to Eat	The World in Your Home				
ABC						[.... Gillette Cavalcade of Sports ....]		

SATURDAY
1946

	7:00	7:30	8:00	8:30	9:00	9:30	10:00	10:30
DUMONT								
CBS								
NBC								
ABC								

SUNDAY
1947

	7:00	7:30	8:00	8:30	9:00	9:30	10:00	10:30
DUMONT								
CBS								
NBC			[·········· Various Special Presentations ··········]					
ABC								

MONDAY
1947

	7:00	7:30	8:00	8:30	9:00	9:30	10:00	10:30
DUMONT	Small Fry Club	Doorway to Fame						
CBS								
NBC			Americana Esso Reporter		[··········· Gillette Cavalcade of Sports ···········]			
ABC								

TUESDAY
1947

	7:00	7:30	8:00	8:30	9:00	9:30	10:00	10:30
DUMONT	Small Fry Club		[·· Western Movie ···]					
CBS								
NBC					Mary Kay and Johnny			
ABC								

WEDNESDAY
1947

	7:00	7:30	8:00	8:30	9:00	9:30	10:00	10:30
DUMONT	Small Fry Club							
CBS								
NBC			Kraft Television [...... Theatre ......]	In the Kelvinator Kitchen				
ABC								

THURSDAY
1947

	7:00	7:30	8:00	8:30	9:00	9:30	10:00	10:30
DUMONT	Small Fry Club	Birthday Party		Charade Quiz				
CBS								
NBC		NBC TV Newsreel	Musical Merry-Go-Round	Eye Witness	You Are an Artist			
ABC								

FRIDAY
1947

	7:00	7:30	8:00	8:30	9:00	9:30	10:00	10:30
DUMONT	Small Fry Club							
CBS								
NBC			Campus Hoopla	The World in Your Home [........... Gillette Cavalcade of Sports ....]				
ABC								

SATURDAY
1947

	7:00	7:30	8:00	8:30	9:00	9:30	10:00	10:30
DUMONT								
CBS								
NBC								
ABC								

SUNDAY
1948

	7:00	7:30	8:00	8:30	9:00	9:30	10:00	10:30
DUMONT	[Original Amateur Hour]							
CBS	Newsweek in Review	[Studio One/Various]		Riddle Me This	[Toast of the Town]		America Speaks	News
NBC	Mary Kay And Johnny News	Welcome Aboard	Author Meets the Critics	Meet the Press	[Philco TV Playhouse]			
ABC	Pauline Fredericks	Southern-aires Quartet	Hollywood Screen Test	Actors' Studio	[........ Movie ....]			

MONDAY
1948

	7:00	7:30	8:00	8:30	9:00	9:30	10:00	10:30
DUMONT	Doorway to Fame	Camera Headlines	Court of Current [........ Issues ....]					
		Champagne and Orchids						
CBS	Places, Please	News	Prize Party	Arthur Godfrey's Talent Scouts	[............... Sporting Events ....]			
		Face the Music						
NBC		American Song	Chevrolet Tele-Theatre	Americana	Newsreel [......... Boxing from St. Nicholas Arena ....]			
		News						
ABC	News	Kiernan's Corner	Quizzing the News	[..... Film Shorts .....]				

TUESDAY
1948

	7:00	7:30	8:00	8:30	9:00	9:30	10:00	10:30
DUMONT					[·············· Sporting Events ··············]			
CBS	Roar of the Rails	News Face the Music	[······· Movie ·······]		We, the People	People's Platform		
NBC		Musical Miniatures News	[Texaco Star Theatre]		Mary Margaret McBride	News/Films	[··· Wrestling from St. Nicholas ···] Arena	
ABC	News	Movieland Quiz	Film Shorts	[··· America's Town Meeting ···] of the air				

WEDNESDAY
1948

	7:00	7:30	8:00	8:30	9:00	9:30	10:00	10:30
DUMONT	Birthday Party	Camera Headlines Film Shorts	Photographic Horizons	The Growing Paynes	[............ Boxing from Jamaica Arena ....]			
CBS	Places, Please	News Face the Music	Kobbs Korner	Winner Take All	[..... Pabst Blue Ribbon Boxing .....]		News	
NBC		You Are an Artist News	Girl About Town Picture This	Ted Steele Story of the Week	Kraft Television [........ Theatre ....]		Newsreel [.... Village Barn ....]	
ABC	News	Critic at Large	Gay Nineties Revue	Film Shorts Three About Town	[........ Wrestling from Washington, D.C. ....]			

THURSDAY
1948

	7:00	7:30	8:00	8:30	9:00	9:30	10:00	10:30
DUMONT	Adventures of Okey Dokey	Camera Headlines	Film Shorts	Charade Quiz	[............ Sporting Events ....]			
CBS		News / Face the Music	To the Queen's Taste	[............ Movies/Sports ....]				
NBC	Paris Caval-cade of Fashion	Musical Miniatures / Sportsman of the Week / News	NBC Pre-sents / The Nature of Things	Swift Show	Gulf Road Show with Bob Smith	Bigelow Show		
ABC	News / Film Shorts	Local	Fashion Story	Club Seven	[............ Movie ....]			

FRIDAY
1948

	7:00	7:30	8:00	8:30	9:00	9:30	10:00	10:30
DUMONT	Key to the Missing	Camera Headlines Film Shorts	Fashions on Parade	Film Shorts	[·············· Sporting Events ···············]			
CBS	Your Sports Special Places, Please	News Face the Music	Sportsman's Quiz What's It Worth?	Capt. Billy's Mississippi Music Hall				
NBC		Musical Merry-Go-Round News	Musical Miniatures	Stop Me If You've Heard This One	I'd Like to See News	[··· Gillette Cavalcade of Sports ···]		
ABC	News	Tales of the Red Caboose Film Shorts	Teenage Book Club	(Various)	Break the Bank	[·············· Local ··············]		

SATURDAY
1948

	7:00	7:30	8:00	8:30	9:00	9:30	10:00	10:30
DUMONT								
CBS			[.... Sporting Events ....]					
NBC		Television Screen Magazine	Saturday Night Jamboree	[................................ Sporting Events ....]				
ABC	News Film Short	Sports with Joe Hasel	Play the Game	Film Shorts	[...................... Sporting Events ....]			

SUNDAY
1949

	7:00	7:30	8:00	8:30	9:00	9:30	10:00	10:30
DUMONT	[........ Front Row Center ....]		Chicagoland Mystery Players	Cinema Varieties	[..	Cross Question ...]		
CBS	Tonight on Broadway	This Is Show Business	[........ Toast of the Town ....]		[........	Fred Waring Show ....]	News	
NBC	Leave It to the Girls	Aldrich Family	Chesterfield Supper Club	Colgate Theatre	Philco TV Playhouse]		Garroway at Large	
ABC	Paul Whiteman's Goodyear Review	ABC Penthouse Players	Think Fast	The Little Revue	[Let There Be Stars]		Celebrity Time	Youth on the March

MONDAY
1949

	7:00	7:30	8:00	8:30	9:00	9:30	10:00	10:30
DUMONT	Captain Video	Manhattan Spotlight Vincent Lopez	Newsweek Views the News	Al Morgan	And Everything Nice	[············	Wrestling ···········]	
CBS	Roar of the Rails	News Sonny Kendis / Herb Shriner Show	Silver Theatre	Arthur Godfrey's Talent Scouts	Candid Camera	The Goldbergs	[····· Studio One ·····]	
NBC	Kukla, Fran and Ollie	Mohawk Showroom News	Chevrolet Theatre	Voice of Firestone	Lights Out	Cities Service Band of America	Quiz Kids	
ABC	[············ Local ············]			Author Meets the Critics	Mr. Black	[·········	Sporting Events ·········]	

TUESDAY
1949

	7:00	7:30	8:00	8:30	9:00	9:30	10:00	10:30
DUMONT	Captain Video	Vincent Lopez	[........ Court of Current Issues ....]		The O'Neills	[..........	Feature Theatre ....]	
CBS	Strictly for Laughs	Sonny Kendis News / Herb Shri-ner Show	[.. Movies/Specials .]		Actors' Stu-dio	Suspense	This Week in Sports	
NBC	Kukla, Fran and Ollie	Mohawk Showroom News	[Texaco Star Theatre]		Fireside Theatre	Life of Riley	[Original Amateur Hour]	
ABC	[..................	News	Local		................]	On Trial	[.. Sporting Events ..]	

WEDNESDAY
1949

	7:00	7:30	8:00	8:30	9:00	9:30	10:00	10:30
DUMONT	Captain Video	Manhattan Spotlight Vincent Lo-pez	[........ Movies ......]		The Plain-clothesman	Famous Jury Trials	Sporting Events ....]	
CBS	Strictly for Laughs	News At Home	Arthur Godfrey and His [....... Friends ....]		Bigelow Show	[.........	Sporting Events ....]	
NBC	Kukla, Fran and Ollie	Mohawk Showroom News	Crisis	The Clock	Kraft Television [....... Theatre ....]		Break the Bank	
ABC	[........ Local ....]		Photoplay Time	Look Photo-crime	Author Meets the Critics	[.........	Sporting Events ....]	

THURSDAY
1949

	7:00	7:30	8:00	8:30	9:00	9:30	10:00	10:30
DUMONT	Captain Video	Manhattan Spotlight Vincent Lopez	[.. Mystery Theatre .]		Morey Amsterdam Show	[..........	Sporting Events ....]	
CBS	Dione Lucas	News Sonny Kendis Herb Shriner Show	Front Page	Inside USA Romance	Ed Wynn Show	[............. Movie ....]		
NBC	Kukla, Fran and Ollie	Mohawk Showroom News	Hollywood Premiere	Mary Kay and Johnny	[Fireball Fun for All]		Martin Kane, Private Eye	[Local]
ABC	Lone Ranger		[.. Stop the Music ..]		Crusade in Europe	Starring Boris Karloff	[... Roller Derby ...]	

FRIDAY
1949

	7:00	7:30	8:00	8:30	9:00	9:30	10:00	10:30
DUMONT	Captain Video	Manhattan Spotlight Vincent Lopez	Hands of Mystery	Headline Clues	Fishing and Hunting Club	Film	[.. Sporting Events .]	
CBS	Strictly for Laughs	News Sonny Kendis Herb Shriner Show	Mama	Man Against Crime	Ford Theatre/54th St. Revue [.......]		People's Platform	Capitol Cloakroom
NBC	Kukla, Fran and Ollie	Mohawk Showroom News	One Man's Family	We, the People	Bonny Maid Versatile Varieties	Big Story/Various	Gillette Cavalcade of Sports [.......]	
ABC	[...... Movie ......]		Majority Rules	Blind Date	Auctionaire	Fun for the Money	[.... Roller Derby ....]	

SATURDAY
1949

	7:00	7:30	8:00	8:30	9:00	9:30	10:00	10:30
DUMONT			[.. Spin the Picture ..]		[.. Cavalcade of Stars]		[.. Sporting Events .]	
CBS		Quincy Howe—News / Blues by Bargy / Herb Shriner Show	Winner Take All	[............. Premiere Playhouse ....]				
NBC		The Nature of Things / News	Twenty Questions	Sessions / Stud's Place	Who Said That?	Meet the Press	Black Robe	
ABC		Hollywood Screen Test	Paul Whiteman's TV / [...... Teen Club ......]		[............. Roller Derby ....]			

SUNDAY
1950

	7:00	7:30	8:00	8:30	9:00	9:30	10:00	10:30
DUMONT	[. . . . . Starlit Time . . .]		Rhythm Rodeo		[Arthur Murray Party]		[They Stand Accused]	
CBS	Gene Autry Show	This Is Show Business	[. . Toast of the Town]		[. Fred Waring Show]		Celebrity Time	What's My Line?
NBC	Leave It to the Girls	Aldrich Family	[Colgate Comedy Hour]		[Philco TV Playhouse]		Garroway at Large	Take a Chance
ABC	Paul Whiteman's Revue	Showtime, USA	Hollywood Premiere Theatre	Sit or Miss	Soap Box Theatre	Marshall Plan in Action	Old Fashioned Meeting	Youth on the March

MONDAY
1950

	7:00	7:30	8:00	8:30	9:00	9:30	10:00	10:30
DUMONT	Captain Video	Susan Raye Manhattan Spotlight	Visit with the Armed Forces	Al Morgan	[............... Sporting Events ....]			
CBS	Stork Club	Perry Como	Lux Video Theatre	Arthur Godfrey's Talent Scouts	Horace Heidt Show	The Goldbergs	[..... Studio One .....]	
NBC	Kukla, Fran and Ollie	Mohawk Showroom	Speidel Show	Voice of Firestone	Lights Out	Robert Montgomery Presents Lucky Strike Time/Musical Comedy Time [........ Time ....]		Who Said That?
ABC	Club Seven	Hollywood Screen Test	Treasury Men in Action	Dick Tracy	College Bowl	On Trial	[... Feature Film ....]	

TUESDAY
1950

	7:00	7:30	8:00	8:30	9:00	9:30	10:00	10:30
DUMONT	Captain Video	Joan Edwards	Court of Current Issues	Johns Hopkins Science Review	[Cavalcade of Bands]		[...... Star Time ......]	
CBS	Stork Club	Faye Emerson	[Presidential Family Playhouse/Sure as Fate]		Vaughn Monroe Musical Variety	Suspense	Danger	We Take Your Word
NBC	Kukla, Fran and Ollie	Little Show	[Texaco Star Theatre]		Firestone Theatre	Circle Theatre	[Original Amateur Hour]	
ABC	Club Seven	Beulah	Game of the Week	Buck Rogers	Billy Rose Show	Can You Top This?	Life Begins at Eighty	Roller Derby

WEDNESDAY
1950

	7:00	7:30	8:00	8:30	9:00	9:30	10:00	10:30
DUMONT	Captain Video	Most Important People / Manhattan Spotlight			Famous Jury Trials	The Plain-clothesman	Broadway to Hollywood	
CBS	Stork Club	Perry Como	[...... Arthur Godfrey and His Friends ......]		[... Teller of Tales ..]		[..... Pabst Blue Ribbon Bouts ...]	
NBC	Kukla, Fran and Ollie		[.. Four Star Revue .]		[...... Kraft Television Theatre ......]		Break the Bank	Stars over Hollywood
ABC	Club Seven	Chance of a Lifetime	[... First Nighter ....]		[......... Don McNeill's TV Club ....]		[... Sporting Events .]	

THURSDAY
1950

	7:00	7:30	8:00	8:30	9:00	9:30	10:00	10:30
DUMONT	Captain Video	Joan Edwards Manhattan Spotlight	[..	Show Goes On ..]	Adventures of Ellery Queen	[.........	Sporting Events ....]	
CBS	Stork Club	Faye Emerson			Alan Young Show	Big Town	Truth or Consequences	Nash Airflyte Theatre
NBC	Kukla, Fran and Ollie	Little Show	You Bet Your Life (Groucho Marx)	Hawkins Falls	Kay Kyser's Kollege of [. Musical Knowledge]		Martin Kane, Private Eye	Wayne King
ABC	Club Seven	Lone Ranger	[..	Stop the Music ..]	Holiday Hotel	Blind Date	I Cover Times Square	Roller Derby

FRIDAY
1950

	7:00	7:30	8:00	8:30	9:00	9:30	10:00	10:30
DUMONT	Captain Video	Most Important People Manhattan Spotlight		Hold that Camera	Hands of Mystery	Inside Detective	[. Cavalcade of Stars]	
CBS	Stork Club	Perry Como	Mama	Man Against Crime	Ford Theatre/Magnavox Theatre [.......]		Morton Downey Show	Beat the Clock
NBC	Kukla, Fran and Ollie	Mohawk Showroom	Quiz Kids	We, the People	Bonny Maid Versatile Varieties	Big Story/The Clock	Gillette Cavalcade of Sports [.......]	
ABC	Club Seven	Life with Linkletter	Twenty Questions	Pro Football Highlights	Pulitzer Prize Playhouse [.......]		Penthouse Party	Stud's Place

SATURDAY
1950

	7:00	7:30	8:00	8:30	9:00	9:30	10:00	10:30
DUMONT	Captain Video		[.... Country Style ..]				Fights ....]	
CBS	Big Top	Week in Review / Faye Emerson	[. Ken Murray Show]		[Frank Sinatra Show]		[.... Sing It Again ....]	
NBC	Hank McCune	One Man's Family	[. Jack Carter Show .]		[...... Your Show of Shows ....]			Your Hit Parade
ABC	Sandy Dreams	Stu Erwin Show	Paul Whiteman's Teen Club [.........]				[................ Roller Derby ....]	

SUNDAY
1951

	7:00	7:30	8:00	8:30	9:00	9:30	10:00	10:30
DUMONT					Rocky King, Detective	The Plain-clothesman	[They Stand Accused]	
CBS	Gene Autry Show	This Is Show Business	[. Toast of the Town]		[. Fred Waring Show]		Goodrich Celebrity Time	What's My Line?
NBC	Chesterfield Sound-Off Time	Young Mr. Bobbin	[Colgate Comedy Hour]		[Philco TV Playhouse]		Red Skelton Show	Leave It to the Girls
ABC	Paul White-man's Goodyear Revue	Music in Velvet	[......... Admission Free ....]			Marshall Plan in Ac-tion	Hour of De-cision	Youth on the March

MONDAY
1951

	7:00	7:30	8:00	8:30	9:00	9:30	10:00	10:30
DUMONT	Captain Video		Stage Entrance	Johns Hopkins Science Review	[················· Wrestling ·················]			
CBS	Local	Perry Como	Lux Video Theatre	Arthur Godfrey's Talent Scouts	I Love Lucy	It's News to Me	[····· Studio One ·····]	
NBC	Kukla, Fran and Ollie	Mohawk Showroom	Speidel Show	Voice of Firestone	Lights Out	Robert Montgomery Presents/Somerset [······ Maugham TV Theatre ······]		
ABC	Local	Hollywood Screen Test	Mr. District Attorney/Amazing Mr. Malone	Life Begins at Eighty	[····· Curtain Up ·····]		Bill Gwinn Show	Stud's Place

TUESDAY
1951

	7:00	7:30	8:00	8:30	9:00	9:30	10:00	10:30
DUMONT	Captain Video		What's the Story	Keep Posted	[Cosmopolitan Theatre]		Hands of Destiny	
CBS	Local	Stork Club	[Frank Sinatra Show]		Crime Syndicated	Suspense	Danger	
NBC	Kukla, Fran and Ollie	Little Show	[Texaco Star Theatre]		Fireside Theatre	Armstrong Circle Theatre	[Original Amateur Hour]	
ABC	Local	Beulah	Charlie Wild, Private Detective	How Did They Get That Way?	United or Not	On Trial		Chicago Symphony

WEDNESDAY
1951

	7:00	7:30	8:00	8:30	9:00	9:30	10:00	10:30
DUMONT	Captain Video				Gallery of Madame Liu-Tsong	Shadow of the Cloak		
CBS	Local	Perry Como	[...... Arthur Godfrey and His Friends ......]		Strike It Rich	The Web	[...... Pabst Blue Ribbon Bouts ......]	
NBC	Kukla, Fran and Ollie	Mohawk Showroom	[...... Kate Smith Evening Hour ......]		[...... Kraft Television Theatre ......]		Break the Bank	Freddy Martin Show
ABC	Local	Chance of a Lifetime	[. Paul Dixon Show .]		Don Mc- Neill's TV Club/Arthur Murray Party	The Clock	[...... Celanese Theatre/King's Crossroads ......]	

THURSDAY
1951

	7:00	7:30	8:00	8:30	9:00	9:30	10:00	10:30
DUMONT	Captain Video		Georgetown University Forum	Broadway to Hollywood	Adventures of Ellery Queen		Bigelow Theatre	
CBS	Local	Stork Club	Burns and Allen Show/ Garry Moore Show	Amos 'n' Andy	Alan Young Show	Big Town	Racquet Squad	Crime Photographer
NBC	Kukla, Fran and Ollie	Little Show	You Bet Your Life (Groucho Marx)	Treasury Men in Action	[... Ford Festival ...]		Martin Kane, Private Eye	Wayne King
ABC	Local	Lone Ranger	[.. Stop the Music ..]		Herb Shriner Show	Gruen Guild Theatre	Paul Dixon Show	

160

FRIDAY
1951

	7:00	7:30	8:00	8:30	9:00	9:30	10:00	10:30
DUMONT	Captain Video		Twenty Questions	You Asked for It	Down You Go	Front Page Detective	[Cavalcade of Sports]	
CBS	Local	Perry Como	Mama	Man Against Crime	Schlitz Playhouse of [........ Stars ....]		Live Like a Millionaire	Hollywood Opening Night
NBC	Kukla, Fran and Ollie	Mohawk Showroom	Quiz Kids	We, the People	Big Story	Aldrich Family	Gillette Cavalcade of [........ Sports ....]	
ABC	Local	Say It with Acting/Life with Linkletter	Mystery Theatre	Stu Erwin Show	Crime with Father	Tales of To-morrow/Versatile Varieties	Dell O'Dell Show	America in View

SATURDAY
1951

	7:00	7:30	8:00	8:30	9:00	9:30	10:00	10:30
DUMONT						[............. Wrestling ....]		
CBS	Sammy Kaye Variety Show	Beat the Clock	[. Ken Murray Show]		Faye Emerson's Wonderful Town	The Show Goes On	[... Songs for Sale ..]	
NBC	American Youth Forum	One Man's Family	[.. All-Star Revue ..]		[....... Your Show of Shows ......]			Your Hit Parade
ABC	Hollywood Theatre Time	Jerry Colonna Show	Paul Whiteman's Teen Club [........ Club ....]		Lesson in Safety	America's Health	[....... Local ....]	

SUNDAY
1952

	7:00	7:30	8:00	8:30	9:00	9:30	10:00	10:30
DUMONT	Georgetown University Forum				Rocky King, Detective	The Plainclothesman	Arthur Murray Show	Youth on the March
CBS	Gene Autry Show	This Is Show Business	[. Toast of the Town]		Fred Waring Show	Break the Bank	The Web	What's My Line?
NBC	Red Skelton Show	Doc Corkle	[Colgate Comedy Hour]		Philco TV Playhouse/ [Goodyear TV Playhouse]		The Doctor	
ABC	You Asked for It	Hot Seat	[... All-Star News ..]		Playhouse #7	This Is Your Life	Hour of Decision	Anywhere USA

MONDAY
1952

	7:00	7:30	8:00	8:30	9:00	9:30	10:00	10:30
DUMONT	Captain Video		Pentagon	Johns Hopkins Science Review	Guide Right	Football Sidelines	[........ Boxing ....]	
CBS	Local	Perry Como	Lux Video Theatre	Arthur Godfrey's Talent Scouts	I Love Lucy	Life with Luigi	[...... Studio One ......]	
NBC	Local	Those Two	What's My Line?	Voice of Firestone	Hollywood Opening Night	Robert Montgomery Presents [........]		Who Said That?
ABC	Local	Hollywood Screen Test	Inspector Mark Saber	United or Not	[... All-Star News ..]	[........ Local ....]		

TUESDAY
1952

	7:00	7:30	8:00	8:30	9:00	9:30	10:00	10:30
DUMONT	Captain Video		Power of Women	Keep Posted	Where Was I?	Quick on the Draw		
CBS		Heaven for Betsy	Leave It to Larry	Red Buttons Show	Crime Syndicated/City Hospital	Suspense	Danger	
NBC		Dinah Shore	[Texaco Star Theatre]		Firestone Theatre	Armstrong Circle Theatre	Two for the Money	Club Embassy
ABC		Beulah	[.............................. Local ....]					

WEDNESDAY
1952

	7:00	7:30	8:00	8:30	9:00	9:30	10:00	10:30
DUMONT	Captain Video	Quarterback Huddle (N.Y. Giants)		Trash or Treasure	[... Stage a Number .]		Pabst Blue Ribbon [........ Fights ....]	
CBS	Local	Perry Como	Arthur Godfrey and His [...... Friends ....]		Strike It Rich	Man Against Crime		
NBC	Local	Those Two	I Married Joan	Scott Music Hall/Cavalcade of America	Kraft Television [....... Theatre ....]		This Is Your Life	
ABC	Local	Name's the Same	[... All-Star News ..]		Adventures of Ellery Queen	[..........]	Sporting Events ....]	

166

THURSDAY
1952

	7:00	7:30	8:00	8:30	9:00	9:30	10:00	10:30
DUMONT	Captain Video				Broadway to Hollywood	Pick the Winner	What's the Story?	Author Meets the Critics
CBS	Local	Heaven for Betsy	Burns and Allen Show	Amos 'n' Andy/Four Star Play-house	Pick the Winner	Big Town	Racquet Squad	I've Got a Secret
NBC	Local	Dinah Shore	You Bet Your Life (Groucho Marx)	Treasury Men in Ac-tion	Dragnet/Gangbusters	Ford Thea-tre	Martin Kane, Pri-vate Eye	
ABC	Local	Lone Ranger	All-Star News	Chance of a Lifetime	Politics on Trial	On Guard	[....... Local ....]	

FRIDAY
1952

	7:00	7:30	8:00	8:30	9:00	9:30	10:00	10:30
DUMONT	Captain Video		Steve Randall	Dark of Night	Life Begins at Eighty		Twenty Questions	Down You Go
CBS	Local	Perry Como	Mama	My Friend Irma	Schlitz Playhouse of Stars	Our Miss Brooks	Mr. and Mrs. North	
NBC	Local	Those Two	RCA Victor Show	Gulf Playhouse	Big Story	Aldrich Family	Gillette Cavalcade of [........ Sports ....]	
ABC	Local	Stu Erwin Show	Adventures of Ozzie and Harriet	[... All-Star News ...]		Tales of Tomorrow	[....... Local ....]	

167

SATURDAY
1952

	7:00	7:30	8:00	8:30	9:00	9:30	10:00	10:30
DUMONT		Pet Shop				[............ Wrestling ....]		Battle of the Ages
CBS	Stork Club	Beat the Clock	[Jackie Gleason Show]		Jane Froman's U.S.A. Canteen	Meet Millie	Balance Your Budget/Quiz Kids	
NBC	Mr. Wizard	My Little Margie	[... All-Star Revue ...]		[Your Show of Shows]		[.. Your Hit Parade .]	
ABC	Paul Whiteman's TV Teen Club	Live Like a Millionaire	[............ Feature Playhouse ....]				[....... Local ....]	

SUNDAY
1953

	7:00	7:30	8:00	8:30	9:00	9:30	10:00	10:30
DUMONT	Georgetown University Forum	Washington Exclusive			Rocky King, Detective	The Plain-clothesman	Dollar a Second	Man Against Crime
CBS	Quiz Kids	Jack Benny/Private Secretary	[. Toast of the Town]		G.E. Theatre/Fred Waring Show	Man Behind the Badge	The Web	What's My Line?
NBC	Paul Winchell Show	Mr. Peepers	[Colgate Comedy Hour]		Philco TV Playhouse/ [Goodyear TV Playhouse]		Letter to Loretta	Man Against Crime
ABC	You Asked for It	Frank Leahy Show	[.. Sporting Events .]		Walter Winchell Show	[. Peter Potter Show .]		Hour of Decision

MONDAY
1953

	7:00	7:30	8:00	8:30	9:00	9:30	10:00	10:30
DUMONT	Captain Video		Twenty Questions	Big Issue	[·············· Sporting Events ··············]			
CBS	Local	Perry Como	Burns and Allen Show	Arthur Godfrey's Talent Scouts	I Love Lucy	Red Buttons Show	[····· Studio One ·····]	
NBC	Local	Arthur Murray Party	Name that Tune	Voice of Firestone	RCA Victor Show Starring Dennis Day	Robert Montgomery [······ Presents ······]		Who Said That?
ABC	Walter Winchell	Jamie	Sky King	Of Many Things	Junior Press Conference	Big Picture	This Is Your Life	Local

TUESDAY
1953

	7:00	7:30	8:00	8:30	9:00	9:30	10:00	10:30
DUMONT	Captain Video		Life Is Worth Living	Pantomime Quiz				
CBS	Local	Jane Froman	Gene Autry Show	Red Skelton Show	This Is Show Business	Suspense	Danger	See It Now
NBC	Local	Dinah Shore	[. Buick-Berle Show .]		Fireside Theatre	Armstrong Circle Theatre	Judge for Yourself	On the Line with Considine
ABC	Local	Cavalcade of America	[...... Local ......]		Make Room for Daddy	U.S. Steel Hour/Motorola [..... TV Theatre .....]		Name's the Same

WEDNESDAY
1953

	7:00	7:30	8:00	8:30	9:00	9:30	10:00	10:30
DUMONT	Captain Video		Johns Hopkins Science Review	Joseph Schildkraut Presents	Colonel Humphrey Flack	On Your Way	Stars on Parade	Music Show
CBS	Local	Perry Como	Arthur Godfrey and His [....... Friends ....]		Strike It Rich	I've Got a Secret	[....... Boxing ......]	
NBC	Local	Coke Time/ News	I Married Joan	My Little Margie	Kraft Television [....... Theatre ....]		This Is Your Life .] [.	
ABC	Local	Inspector Mark Saber	At Issue	America in View	[................ Sporting Events ....]			

THURSDAY
1953

	7:00	7:30	8:00	8:30	9:00	9:30	10:00	10:30
DUMONT	Captain Video		N.Y. Giants Quarterback Huddle	Broadway to Hollywood	What's the Story?			
CBS	Local	Jane Froman	Meet Mr. McNutley	Four Star Playhouse	Lux Video Theatre	Big Town	Philip Morris Playhouse	Place the Face
NBC	Local	Dinah Shore	You Bet Your Life (Groucho Marx)	Treasury Men in Action	Dragnet	Ford Theatre	Martin Kane, Private Eye	Local
ABC	Local	Lone Ranger	Quick as a Flash	Where's Raymond?	Back that Fact	Kraft Television Theatre [.......]		Local

FRIDAY
1953

	7:00	7:30	8:00	8:30	9:00	9:30	10:00	10:30
DUMONT			Front Page Detective	Melody Street	Life Begins at Eighty	Nine-Thirty Curtain	Chance of a Lifetime	Down You Go
CBS	Local	Perry Como	Mama	Topper	Schlitz Playhouse of Stars	Our Miss Brooks	My Friend Irma	Person to Person
NBC	Local	Coke Time	Dave Garroway Show	Life of Riley	Big Story	Campbell Soundstage	[······· Gillette Cavalcade of Sports ······]	
ABC	Local	Stu Erwin Show	Adventures of Ozzie and Harriet	Pepsi-Cola Playhouse	Pride of the Family	Comeback Story	[·. Showcase Theatre]	

SATURDAY
1953

	7:00	7:30	8:00	8:30	9:00	9:30	10:00	10:30
DUMONT								
CBS	Meet Millie	Beat the Clock	[Jackie Gleason Show]		Two for the Money	My Favorite Husband	Medallion Theatre	Revlon Mirror Theatre
NBC	Mr. Wizard	Ethel and Albert	Bonino	Original Amateur Hour	[...... Your Show of Shows ......]			Your Hit Parade
ABC	Paul Whiteman's TV Teen Club	Leave It to the Girls	Talent Patrol	Music at the Meadowbrook	[...... Fights ......]		Madison Square Garden Highlights	Local

SUNDAY
1954

	7:00	7:30	8:00	8:30	9:00	9:30	10:00	10:30
DUMONT	Author Meets the Critics	Opera Cameos			Rocky King, Detective	Life Begins at Eighty	Music Show	
CBS	Lassie	Jack Benny/ Private Secretary	[. Toast of the Town]		G.E. Theatre	Honestly Celeste	Father Knows Best	What's My Line?
NBC	People Are Funny	Mr. Peepers	[Colgate Comedy Hour]		Philco TV Playhouse/ Goodyear TV [...... Playhouse ......]		Loretta Young Show	The Hunter
ABC	You Asked for It	Pepsi-Cola Playhouse	Flight Number 7	Big Picture	Walter Winchell/Martha Wright	Dr. I.Q.	Break the Bank	Local

MONDAY
1954

	7:00	7:30	8:00	8:30	9:00	9:30	10:00	10:30
DUMONT	Captain Video		Ilona Massey Show		[.............. Sporting Events ....]			
CBS	Local	Perry Como	Burns and Allen Show	Arthur Godfrey's Talent Scouts	I Love Lucy	December Bride	[..... Studio One .....]	
NBC	Local	Tony Martin/News	[.... Caesar's Hour ..]		Medic	[... Robert Montgomery Presents ...]		
ABC	Kukla, Fran and Ollie	Name's the Same	Come Closer	Come Closer	Voice of Firestone	Junior Press Conference	[... Sporting Events .]	

TUESDAY
1954

	7:00	7:30	8:00	8:30	9:00	9:30	10:00	10:30
DUMONT	Captain Video		Life Is Worth Living	Studio 57	One Minute Please			
CBS	Local	Jo Stafford	Red Skelton Show	Halls of Ivy	Meet Millie	Danger	Life with Father	See It Now
NBC	Local	Dinah Shore	[. Buick-Berle Show .]		Fireside Theatre	Armstrong Circle Theatre	Truth or Consequences	It's a Great Life
ABC	Kukla, Fran and Ollie	Cavalcade of America	Local	Twenty Questions	Make Room for Daddy	U.S. Steel Hour/Elgin TV [........ Hour ....]		Stop the Music

WEDNESDAY
1954

	7:00	7:30	8:00	8:30	9:00	9:30	10:00	10:30
DUMONT	Captain Video				[Chicago Symphony]		Down You Go	
CBS	Local	Perry Como	Arthur Godfrey and His Friends [........]		Strike It Rich	I've Got a Secret	Pabst Blue Ribbon Bouts [........]	
NBC	Local	Coke Time	I Married Joan	My Little Margie	Kraft Television Theatre [........]		This Is Your Life	Big Town
ABC	Kukla, Fran and Ollie	[..... Disneyland .....]		Stu Erwin Show	Masquerade Party	Enterprise USA	[........ Local ....]	

THURSDAY
1954

	7:00	7:30	8:00	8:30	9:00	9:30	10:00	10:30
DUMONT	Captain Video		[They Stand Accused]		What's the Story?			
CBS		Local	Ray Milland Show	[...... Climax ......]		Four Star Playhouse	Public Defender	Name that Tune
NBC		Local	You Bet Your Life (Groucho Marx)	Justice	Dragnet	Ford Theatre	[Lux Video Theatre]	
ABC	Kukla, Fran and Ollie	Lone Ranger	Mail Story	Treasury Men in Action	So You Want to Lead a Band	[...... Kraft Television Theatre ......]		

FRIDAY
1954

	7:00	7:30	8:00	8:30	9:00	9:30	10:00	10:30
DUMONT	Captain Video				The Stranger		Chance of a Lifetime	Time Will Tell
CBS	Local	Perry Como	Mama	Topper	Schlitz Playhouse of the Stars	Our Miss Brooks	The Lineup	Person to Person
NBC	Local	Dinah Shore/Coke Time	Red Buttons Show	Life of Riley	Big Story	Dear Phoebe	Gillette Cavalcade of [........ Sports ....]	
ABC	Kukla, Fran and Ollie	Adventures of Rin Tin Tin	Adventures of Ozzie and Harriet	Ray Bolger Show	Dollar a Second	The Vise	[........ Local ....]	

SATURDAY 1954

	7:00	7:30	8:00	8:30	9:00	9:30	10:00	10:30
DUMONT			[·············· Sporting Events ··············]					
CBS	Gene Autry Show	Beat the Clock	[Jackie Gleason Show]		Two for the Money	My Favorite Husband	That's My Boy	Willy
NBC	Mr. Wizard	Ethel and Albert	Mickey Rooney Show	Place the Face	Imogene Coca Show	Texaco Star Theatre	George Gobel Show	Your Hit Parade
ABC	Local	Compass	[· Dotty Mack Show ·]		[·· Sporting Events ·]		Stork Club	

SUNDAY 1955

	7:00	7:30	8:00	8:30	9:00	9:30	10:00	10:30
CBS	Lassie	Jack Benny/Private Secretary	[········ Toast of the Town ········]		G.E. Theatre	Alfred Hitchcock Presents	$64,000 Challenge	What's My Line?
NBC	It's a Great Life	Frontier	[Colgate Comedy Hour]		[···· TV Theatre ····]		Loretta Young Show	Justice
ABC	You Asked for It	[······· Famous Film Festival ·······]			Chance of a Lifetime	Original Amateur Hour	Life Begins at Eighty	

MONDAY 1955

	7:00	7:30	8:00	8:30	9:00	9:30	10:00	10:30
CBS	Local	Adventures of Robin Hood	Burns and Allen Show	Arthur Godfrey Talent Scouts	I Love Lucy	December Bride	[..... Studio One .....]	
NBC	Local	Tony Martin Show	[..... Sid Caesar .....]		Medic	[.... Robert Montgomery Presents ...]		
ABC	Kukla, Fran and Ollie	Topper	TV Reader's Digest	Voice of Firestone	Dotty Mack Show	Medical Horizons	Big Picture	Local

TUESDAY 1955

	7:00	7:30	8:00	8:30	9:00	9:30	10:00	10:30
CBS	Local	Name that Tune	Navy Log	You'll Never Get Rich	Meet Millie	Red Skelton Show	$64,000 Question	My Favorite Husband
NBC	Local	Dinah Shore (15 Min.)	[... Milton Berle ....]		Fireside Theatre	Armstrong Circle [...... Theatre ......]		Big Town
ABC	Kukla, Fran and Ollie	Warner Brothers [...... Presents ......]		Life and Legend of Wyatt Earp	Make Room for Daddy	DuPont Cavalcade [...... Theatre ......]		

WEDNESDAY 1955

	7:00	7:30	8:00	8:30	9:00	9:30	10:00	10:30
CBS	Local	Brave Eagle	Arthur Godfrey and His Friends	[........]	The Million-aire	I've Got a Secret	20th-Century Fox/U.S. Steel Hour	[.....]
NBC	Local	Eddie Fisher (15 min.)	Screen Director's Playhouse	Father Knows Best	Kraft Television Theatre	[........]	This Is Your Life	Douglas Fairbanks Presents
ABC	Kukla, Fran and Ollie	[..... Disneyland .....]		MGM Parade	Masquerade Party	Break the Bank	[.. Sporting Events .]	

THURSDAY 1955

	7:00	7:30	8:00	8:30	9:00	9:30	10:00	10:30
CBS	Local	Sergeant Preston of the Yukon	Bob Cummings Show	[...... Climax ......]		Four Star Playhouse	Johnny Carson Show	Wanted
NBC	Local	Dinah Shore	You Bet Your Life	People's Choice	Dragnet	[........]	Lux Video Theatre	[........]
ABC	Kukla, Fran and Ollie	Lone Ranger	Life Is Worth Living	Stop the Music	Star Tonight	Down You Go	Outside the U.S.A.	Local

FRIDAY 1955

	7:00	7:30	8:00	8:30	9:00	9:30	10:00	10:30
CBS	Local	Adventures of Champion	Mama	Our Miss Brooks	The Crusader	Schlitz Playhouse of Stars	The Lineup	Person to Person
NBC	Local	Coke Time	Truth or Consequences	Life of Riley	Big Story	Dear Phoebe (Peter Lawford)	[........ Gillette Cavalcade of Sports ....]	
ABC	Kukla, Fran and Ollie	Adventures of Rin Tin Tin	Adventures of Ozzie and Harriet	Crossroads	Dollar a Second	The Vise	Ethel and Albert	Local

SATURDAY 1955

	7:00	7:30	8:00	8:30	9:00	9:30	10:00	10:30
CBS	Gene Autry	Beat the Clock	Stage Show	The Honeymooners	Herb Shriner	It's Always Jan	Gunsmoke	Damon Runyon Theatre
NBC	Local	Big Surprise	Perry Como	People Are Funny	Jimmy Durante	George Gobel	Your Hit Parade	
ABC	Local	[......... Ozark Jamboree ....]			[Lawrence Welk Show]		Tomorrow's Careers	Local

SUNDAY 1956

	7:00	7:30	8:00	8:30	9:00	9:30	10:00	10:30
CBS	Lassie	Jack Benny/ Private Secretary	[. Ed Sullivan Show .]		G.E. Theatre	Alfred Hitchcock Presents	$64,000 Challenge	What's My Line?
NBC	Tales of The 77th Bengal Lancers	Circus Boy	[. Steve Allen Show .]		Goodyear Theatre/Alcoa [........ Hour ....]		Loretta Young Show	Bowling
ABC	You Asked for It	Ted Mack Amateur [......... Hour ....]		Press Conference	[.............. Omnibus ....]			

MONDAY 1956

	7:00	7:30	8:00	8:30	9:00	9:30	10:00	10:30
CBS	Local	Adventures of Robin Hood	Burns and Allen Show	Godfrey Talent Scouts	I Love Lucy	December Bride	[...... Studio One .....]	
NBC	Local	Nat "King" Cole Show	Sir Lancelot	Stanley	Medic	[.... Robert Montgomery Presents ...]		
ABC	Kukla, Fran and Ollie	Bold Journey	Danny Thomas Show	Voice of Firestone	Life Is Worth Living	[....... Lawrence Welk Show ....]		

TUESDAY 1956

	7:00	7:30	8:00	8:30	9:00	9:30	10:00	10:30
CBS	Local	Name that Tune	Phil Silvers	The Brothers	Herb Shriner	Red Skelton	$64,000 Question	Do You Trust Your Wife?
NBC	Sporting Events	Jonathan Winters (15 min.)	Big Surprise	Noah's Ark	Jane Wyman Show	[...... Armstrong Circle Theatre ......]		Break the Bank
ABC	Kukla, Fran and Ollie (15 min.)	[.. Conflict/Cheyenne]		Life and Legend of Wyatt Earp	Broken Arrow	DuPont Theatre	It's Polka Time	Local

WEDNESDAY 1956

	7:00	7:30	8:00	8:30	9:00	9:30	10:00	10:30
CBS	Local	Giant Step	[Arthur Godfrey Show]		The Millionaire	I've Got a Secret	20th Century Fox Hour/ [.. U.S. Steel Hour ..]	
NBC	Local	Eddie Fisher Show	Adventures of Hiram Holiday	Father Knows Best	[...... Kraft Television Theatre ......]		This Is Your Life	Twenty-One
ABC	Kukla, Fran and Ollie (15 min.)	[..... Disneyland .....]		Navy Log	Adventures of Ozzie and Harriet	Ford Theater	[.. Sporting Events .]	

THURSDAY
1956

	7:00	7:30	8:00	8:30	9:00	9:30	10:00	10:30
CBS	Local	Sergeant Preston of the Yukon	Bob Cummings Show	[...... Climax ......]		[.........	Playhouse 90	.........]
NBC	Local	Dinah Shore News	You Bet Your Life	Dragnet	People's Choice	Tennessee Ernie Ford Show	[Lux Video Theatre]	
ABC	Kukla, Fran and Ollie (15 min.)	Lone Ranger	[.... Circus Time ....]		] [... Wire Service ...]		[... Ozark Jubilee ...]	

FRIDAY
1956

	7:00	7:30	8:00	8:30	9:00	9:30	10:00	10:30
CBS	Local	My Friend Flicka	West Point Story	Zane Grey Theatre	Crusader	Schlitz Playhouse	The Lineup	Person to Person
NBC	Local	Eddie Fisher News	Life of Riley	Walter Winchell	On Trial	Big Story	Gillette Cavalcade of [........	Sports ......]
ABC	Kukla, Fran and Ollie (15 min.)	Rin Tin Tin	Jim Bowie	Crossroads	Treasure Hunt	The Vise	[... Ray Anthony ...]	

SATURDAY
1956

	7:00	7:30	8:00	8:30	9:00	9:30	10:00	10:30
CBS	Beat the Clock	The Buccaneers	[.. Jackie Gleason ..]		Gale Storm Show	Hey, Jeannie	Gunsmoke	High Finance
NBC	Local	People Are Funny	[..... Perry Como ....]		[... Caesar's Hour ..]		George Gobel	Your Hit Parade
ABC	Local	[....... Famous Film Festival ....]			[Lawrence Welk Show]		Masquerade Party	Local

SUNDAY
1957

	7:00	7:30	8:00	8:30	9:00	9:30	10:00	10:30
CBS	Lassie	Bachelor Father	[. Ed Sullivan Show .]		G.E. Theatre	Alfred Hitchcock Presents	$64,000 Challenge	What's My Line?
NBC	Amateur Hour	Sally	[. Steve Allen Show .]		[... Dinah Shore ....]		Loretta Young Show	
ABC	You Asked for It	[...... Maverick ....]		Bowling	Open Hearing	Sporting Events	Scotland Yard	Local

MONDAY 1957

	7:00	7:30	8:00	8:30	9:00	9:30	10:00	10:30
CBS	Burns and Allen Show	Godfrey Talent Scouts	Danny Thomas	[...........	DuPont Show ....]	[........	Film ....]
NBC	Twenty-six Men	The Restless Gun	The Price Is Right	Tales of Wells Fargo	Twenty-One	A Turn of Fate	[...... Suspicion .....]
ABC	Sports Focus	Inner Sanctum	Guy Mitchell	Bold Journey	Voice of Firestone	[... Lawrence Welk ...]	Stars of Jazz

TUESDAY 1957

	7:00	7:30	8:00	8:30	9:00	9:30	10:00	10:30
CBS	Phil Silvers Show	Eve Arden Show	To Tell the Truth	Red Skelton	$64,000 Question	Assignment Foreign Legion	Life with Father	Local
NBC	Boots and Saddles	Nat "King" Cole Show	[... Eddie Fisher ...]	Meet McGraw	Bob Cummings Show	The Californians	Local
ABC	Sports Focus	[Sugarfoot/Cheyenne]	The Life and Legend of Wyatt Earp	Broken Arrow	Telephone Time	West Point Story	Local

WEDNESDAY
1957

	7:00	7:30	8:00	8:30	9:00	9:30	10:00	10:30
CBS	Local	I Love Lucy [..	The Big Record ..]		The Million-aire	I've Got a Secret	Armstrong Circle [Theatre/U.S. Steel Hour]	Local
NBC	Local	[.... Wagon Train ...]		Father Knows Best	Kraft Television [...... Theatre ......]		This Is Your Life	Local
ABC	Local	[.... Disneyland .....]		Tombstone Territory	Adventures of Ozzie and Harriet	Walter Winchell File	Wednesday Night [....... Fights ....]	

THURSDAY
1957

	7:00	7:30	8:00	8:30	9:00	9:30	10:00	10:30
CBS	The Honey-mooners	Men of An-napolis	Harbour-master	[.. Shower of Stars ..]		[............ Playhouse 90 ....]		
NBC	Death Valley Days	Tic Tac Dough	Groucho Marx	Dragnet	People's Choice	Tennessee Ernie Ford Show	Rosemary Clooney	Jane Wyman
ABC	Sports Focus	Circus Boy	Zorro	Real McCoys	Pat Boone Show	O.S.S.	Navy Log	Local

FRIDAY 1957

	7:00	7:30	8:00	8:30	9:00	9:30	10:00	10:30
CBS	Local	Leave It to Beaver	Trackdown	Dick Powell's Zane Grey Theatre	Mr. Adams and Eve	Schlitz Playhouse	The Lineup	Person to Person
NBC	Local	Saber of London	Court of Last Resort	Life of Riley	M Squad	The Thin Man	[....... Gillette Cavalcade of Sports ....]	
ABC	Local	Rin Tin Tin	Jim Bowie	Patrice Munsel Show	Frank Sinatra Show	Date with the Angels	Colt .45	Local

SATURDAY 1957

	7:00	7:30	8:00	8:30	9:00	9:30	10:00	10:30
CBS	Local	[... Perry Mason ...]		Dick and the Duchess	Gale Storm Show	Have Gun Will Travel	Gunsmoke	Local
NBC	Local	People Are Funny	[..... Perry Como ....]		Polly Bergen Show	[...... Gisele MacKenzie Show ....]		Your Hit Parade
ABC	Local	Keep It in the Family	[Country Music Jubilee]		[.. Lawrence Welk ..]		Mike Wallace Interviews	Local

SUNDAY 1958

	7:00	7:30	8:00	8:30	9:00	9:30	10:00	10:30
CBS	Lassie	Bachelor Father	[. Ed Sullivan Show .]		G.E. Theatre	Alfred Hitchcock	$64,000 Question	What's My Line?
NBC	Saber of London	Northwest Passage	[. Steve Allen Show .]		[.... Dinah Shore ....]		Loretta Young Show	Film
ABC	You Asked for It	[...... Maverick ......]		Lawman	Colt .45	[..... Encounter .....]		Music Is My Beat

MONDAY 1958

	7:00	7:30	8:00	8:30	9:00	9:30	10:00	10:30
CBS	Local	Name that Tune	The Texan	Father Knows Best	Danny Thomas Show	Ann Sothern Show	[. Desilu Playhouse .]	
NBC	Local	Tic Tac Dough	Restless Gunn	Tales of Wells Fargo	Peter Gunn	Alcoa Theatre	Arthur Murray Party	Local
ABC	Local	[... Jubilee U.S.A. ...]		Bold Journey	Voice of Firestone	Anybody Can Play	This Is Music	Local

TUESDAY 1958

	7:00	7:30	8:00	8:30	9:00	9:30	10:00	10:30
CBS	Local	Stars in Action	Keep Talking	To Tell the Truth	Arthur Godfrey Show	Red Skelton	[Garry Moore Show]	
NBC	Local	Dragnet	[....... Eddie Fisher/George Gobel ....]		George Burns	Bob Cummings Show	The Californians	African Patrol
ABC	Local	[Sugarfoot/Cheyenne]		Life and Legend of Wyatt Earp	The Rifleman	Naked City	Confession	Local

WEDNESDAY 1958

	7:00	7:30	8:00	8:30	9:00	9:30	10:00	10:30
CBS	Local	Twilight Theatre	[....... Pursuit ....]		The Millionaire	I've Got a Secret	[Armstrong Circle Theatre/Alcoa Theatre]	
NBC	Local	[.... Wagon Train ....]		The Price Is Right	Milton Berle	Bat Masterson	This Is Your Life	Local
ABC	[.........	Lawrence Welk ....]		Adventures of Ozzie and Harriet	Donna Reed Show	Patti Page Show	[........ Wednesday Night Fights ....]	

THURSDAY
1958

	7:00	7:30	8:00	8:30	9:00	9:30	10:00	10:30
CBS	Local	I Love Lucy	December Bride	Yancy Der-ringer	Dick Powell's Zane Grey Theatre	[············ Playhouse 90 ············]		
NBC	Local	Jefferson Drum	Ed Wynn Show	Twenty-One	Behind Closed Doors	Tennessee Ernie Ford Show	You Bet Your Life	Masquerade Party
ABC	Local	Leave it to Beaver	Zorro	The Real McCoys	Pat Boone Show	Rough Riders	Traffic Court	Local

FRIDAY
1958

	7:00	7:30	8:00	8:30	9:00	9:30	10:00	10:30
CBS	Local	Your Hit Pa-rade	Trackdown	Jackie Glea-son	Phil Silvers Show	Lux/Schlitz Playhouse	The Lineup	Person to Person
NBC	Local	Buckskin	[··· Ellery Queen ···]		M Squad	The Thin Man	[Cavalcade of Sports]	
ABC	Local	Rin Tin Tin	[·· Disney Presents ·]		Man with a Camera	[·· 77 Sunset Strip ··]		Local

SATURDAY 1958

	7:00	7:30	8:00	8:30	9:00	9:30	10:00	10:30
CBS	Local	[... Perry Mason ...]		Wanted—Dead or Alive	Gale Storm Show	Have Gun Will Travel	Gunsmoke	Local
NBC	Local	People Are Funny	[. Perry Como Show]		Steve Canyon	[... Cimarron City ...]		Brains and Brawn
ABC	Local	Dick Clark Show	[.. Jubilee U.S.A. ...]		[Lawrence Welk Show]		Sammy Kaye	Local

SUNDAY 1959

	7:00	7:30	8:00	8:30	9:00	9:30	10:00	10:30
CBS	Lassie	Dennis the Menace	Ed Sullivan Show .]		G.E. Theatre	Alfred Hitchcock Presents	George Gobel	What's My Line?
NBC	[...... Riverboat ......]		[. Sunday Showcase .]		[.... Dinah Shore ....]		Loretta Young Show	Film
ABC	Colt .45	[...... Maverick .....]		Lawman	The Rebel	[... The Alaskans ....]		World of Talent

MONDAY 1959

	7:00	7:30	8:00	8:30	9:00	9:30	10:00	10:30
CBS	Local	Masquerade Party	The Texan	Father Knows Best	Danny Thomas	Ann Sothern	Hennesey	June Allyson Show
NBC	Local	Richard Diamond	Love and Marriage	Wells Fargo	Peter Gunn	[.......... Hall of Fame ....]		
ABC	Local	[...... Cheyenne .....]		[Bourbon Street Beat]		[Adventures in Paradise]		Man with a Camera

TUESDAY 1959

	7:00	7:30	8:00	8:30	9:00	9:30	10:00	10:30
CBS	News	Film	Dennis O'Keefe	[.............. (Special) ....]			[.... CBS Reports ....]	
NBC	Rescue 8	[...... Laramie ......]		Fibber McGee and Molly	Arthur Murray Party	[...... Startime ......]		Mike Hammer
ABC	Tales of the Vikings	[...... Sugarfoot .....]		Life and Legend of Wyatt Earp	The Rifleman	Philip Marlowe	[.. Alcoa Presents ..]	

WEDNESDAY 1959

	7:00	7:30	8:00	8:30	9:00	9:30	10:00	10:30
CBS	Local	[.... The Lineup ...]		Men into Space	The Million-aire	I've Got a Secret	Circle Theatre/U.S. Steel [....... Hour ....]	
NBC	Local	[.... Wagon Train ...]		The Price Is Right	[..... Perry Como ...]		This Is Your Life	Wichita Town
ABC	Local	Court of Last Resort	Charley Weaver's Hobby Show	Adventures of Ozzie and Harriet	[... Hawaiian Eye ..]		[... Sporting Events .]	

THURSDAY 1959

	7:00	7:30	8:00	8:30	9:00	9:30	10:00	10:30
CBS	News	To Tell the Truth	Betty Hut-ton	Johnny Ringo	Zane Grey Theatre	[............	Playhouse 90	............]
NBC	Death Val-ley Days	Law of the Plainsman	Bat Master-son	Staccato	Bachelor Father	Tennessee Ernie Ford	Groucho Marx	Lawless Years
ABC	This Man Dawson	Gale Storm	Donna Reed Show	The Real McCoys	Pat Boone Show	[. The Untouchables]		Take a Good Look

FRIDAY
1959

	7:00	7:30	8:00	8:30	9:00	9:30	10:00	10:30
CBS	News	[...... Rawhide ......]		Hotel de Paree	[. Desilu Playhouse .]		Twilight Zone	Person to Person
NBC	[...... Boxing ......]		[...... (Special) ....]		M Squad		People Are Funny	Sea Hunt
ABC	The Honeymooners	[.. Disney Presents .]		Man from Black Hawk	[... 77 Sunset Strip ..]		Robert Taylor's Detectives	Black Saddle

SATURDAY
1959

	7:00	7:30	8:00	8:30	9:00	9:30	10:00	10:30
CBS	News	[... Perry Mason ...]		Wanted Dead or Alive	Mr. Lucky	Have Gun Will Travel	Gunsmoke	Markham
NBC	Silent Search	[...... Bonanza ......]		Man and the Challenge	The Deputy	[..... Five Fingers ...]		It Could Be You
ABC	Lock Up	Dick Clark Show	High Road	Leave It to Beaver	[..... Let's Dance ...]		[.. Jubilee U.S.A. ..]	

200

SUNDAY 1960

	7:00	7:30	8:00	8:30	9:00	9:30	10:00	10:30
CBS	Lassie	Dennis the Menace	[...... (Special) ......]		G.E. Theatre	Jack Benny	Candid Camera	What's My Line?
NBC	[.. Shirley Temple ..]		National Velvet	Tab Hunter	[... Dinah Shore ....]		Loretta Young Show	This Is Your Life
ABC	Walt Disney Presents	[...... Maverick ......]		Lawman	The Rebel	[...........	The Islanders	.........]

MONDAY 1960

	7:00	7:30	8:00	8:30	9:00	9:30	10:00	10:30
CBS	The Case of the Dangerous Robin	To Tell the Truth	Pete and Gladys	Bringing Up Buddy	Danny Thomas	Andy Griffith	Hennesey	News
NBC	Manhunt	[...... Riverboat ......]		(Special)	Klondike	Dante	Barbara Stanwyck	Jackpot Bowl
ABC	Mackenzie's Raiders	[...... Cheyenne ......]		[...... Surfside 6 ......]		[Adventures in Paradise]		Peter Gunn

TUESDAY
1960

	7:00	7:30	8:00	8:30	9:00	9:30	10:00	10:30
CBS	Sea Hunt	Jim Backus Show	Father Knows Best	Dobie Gillis	Tom Ewell Show	Red Skelton	[.....	Gary Moore ....]
NBC	Best of the Post	[.....	Laramie ......]	Alfred Hitchcock	[.......	Thriller ......]	[...	Dean Martin ....]
ABC	Expedition	Bugs Bunny	The Rifleman	Life and Legend of Wyatt Earp	[.	Stagecoach West .	Alcoa Presents	Not for Hire

WEDNESDAY
1960

	7:00	7:30	8:00	8:30	9:00	9:30	10:00	10:30
CBS	The Third Man	[.....	Aquanauts .....]	Wanted Dead or Alive	My Sister Eileen	I've Got a Secret	[..	U.S. Steel Hour .]
NBC	Interpol Calling	[...	Wagon Train ....]	News	[....	Perry Como ...]	Peter Loves Mary	Mike Hammer
ABC	Man and the Challenge	[....	Hong Kong ....]	Adventures of Ozzie and Harriet	[...	Hawaiian Eye ..	[......	Naked City .....]

THURSDAY
1960

	7:00	7:30	8:00	8:30	9:00	9:30	10:00	10:30
CBS	Assignment Underwater	[....	The Witness ....]	Zane Grey Theatre	Angel	Ann Sothern	Person to Person	June Allyson
NBC	Death Valley Days	[....	The Outlaws ....]	Bat Masterson	Bachelor Father	Tennessee Ernie Ford	Groucho Marx	Grand Jury
ABC	Glencannon	Guestward Ho!	Donna Reed Show	The Real McCoys	My Three Sons	[. The Untouchables]		Close-up

FRIDAY
1960

	7:00	7:30	8:00	8:30	9:00	9:30	10:00	10:30
CBS	Shotgun Slade	[......	Rawhide ......]	[......	Route 66 ......]	News	Twilight Zone	Eyewitness to History
NBC	Coronado 9	[....	Dan Raven ....]	The Westerner	[. O'Conners Ocean .]		[.. Michael Shayne ..]	
ABC	Tombstone Territory	Matty's Funday Funnies	Harrigan and Son	The Flintstones	[.. 77 Sunset Strip ..]		Robert Taylor's Detectives	The Law and Mr. Jones

SATURDAY
1960

	7:00	7:30	8:00	8:30	9:00	9:30	10:00	10:30
CBS	Lock Up	[..... Perry Mason ....]		[..... Checkmate .....]		News	Gunsmoke	Film
NBC	Flight	[...... Bonanza ......]		The Tall Man	The Deputy	[...... (Special) ......]		Film
ABC	[.. Sporting Events .]		Men into Space	Leave It to Beaver	[..... The Roaring Twenties]		[..... Let's Dance ....]	

SUNDAY
1961

	7:00	7:30	8:00	8:30	9:00	9:30	10:00	10:30
CBS	Lassie	Dennis the Menace	[. Ed Sullivan Show .]		Play	Jack Benny	Candid Camera	What's My Line?
NBC	Bullwinkle	Walt Disney Presents	Car 54, Where Are You?	[...... Bonanza ......]		[........ DuPont Show of the Week ....]		
ABC	Maverick	[... Follow the Sun ...]		Lawman	[...... Bus Stop ......]		[Adventures in Paradise]	

MONDAY 1961

	7:00	7:30	8:00	8:30	9:00	9:30	10:00	10:30
CBS	News	To Tell the Truth	Pete and Gladys	Window on Main Street	Danny Thomas	Andy Griffith	Hennesey	I've Got a Secret
NBC	Shotgun Slade	Everglades	National Velvet	The Price Is Right	[..... 87th Precinct ....]		[....... Thriller ......]	
ABC	Expedition	[...... Cheyenne ......]		The Rifleman	[...... Surfside 6 .....]		[...... Ben Casey .....]	

TUESDAY 1961

	7:00	7:30	8:00	8:30	9:00	9:30	10:00	10:30
CBS	News	Marshal Dillon	Dick Van Dyke	Dobbie Gillis	Red Skelton	Ichabod and Me	[......... Play ....]	
NBC	Phil Silvers Show	[...... Laramie ......]		Alfred Hitchcock Presents	[. Dick Powell Show]		[.. Cain's Hundred ...]	
ABC	Ivanhoe	Bugs Bunny	Bachelor Father	Calvin and the Colonel	[...... New Breed .....]		[...... Play ....]	

WEDNESDAY
1961

	7:00	7:30	8:00	8:30	9:00	9:30	10:00	10:30
CBS	News	The Alvin Show (cartoon)	Father Knows Best	[..... Checkmate .....]		Mrs. G Goes to College	[....... Armstrong Circle Theatre ....]	
NBC	Death Valley Days	[..... Wagon Train ....]		Joey Bishop	[..... Perry Como ....]		Bob Newhart	David Brinkley's Journal
ABC	Shannon	[..... Steve Allen ....]		Top Cat	[..... Hawaiian Eye ...]		[. Seasons of Youth .]	

THURSDAY
1961

	7:00	7:30	8:00	8:30	9:00	9:30	10:00	10:30
CBS	News	[... Frontier Circus ..]		Bob Cummings Show	[..... Investigators ...]		At the Source	The U.N. New Yorker
NBC	Ripcord	[... The Outlaws ...]		[..... Dr. Kildare .....]		Hazel	[Sing Along with Mitch]	
ABC	Two Faces West	Ozzie and Harriet	Donna Reed Show	The Real McCoys	My Three Sons	Margie	[. The Untouchables]	

FRIDAY 1961

	7:00	7:30	8:00	8:30	9:00	9:30	10:00	10:30
CBS	News	[...... Rawhide ......]			Route 66 ......]	Father of the Bride	Twilight Zone	Eyewitness
NBC	Lock Up	[...... International Showtime ......]		[... The Detectives ..]		[... Telephone Hour .]		Frank McGee
ABC	King of Diamonds	Straight-away	The Hatha-ways	The Flint-stones	[... 77 Sunset Strip ...]		Target: The Corruptors	[......]

SATURDAY 1961

	7:00	7:30	8:00	8:30	9:00	9:30	10:00	10:30
CBS	Sea Hunt	[... Perry Mason ...]		[... The Defenders ...]		Have Gun Will Travel	[..... Gunsmoke .....]	
NBC	News	[.... Wells Fargo ...]		The Tall Man	[................. Movies ....]			
ABC	Matty's Funday Funnies	[The Roaring Twenties]		Ernie Kovacs (Special)	[Lawrence Welk Show]		[... Sporting Events .]	

SUNDAY
1962

	7:00	7:30	8:00	8:30	9:00	9:30	10:00	10:30
CBS	Lassie	Dennis the Menace	[. Ed Sullivan Show .]		The Real McCoys	"Play"	Candid Camera	What's My Line?
NBC	Ensign O'Toole	[....... Walt Disney's Wonderful World ....]		Car 54, Where Are You?	[...... Bonanza ......]		[....... DuPont Show of the Week ....]	
ABC	Father Knows Best	The Jetsons	[.............. Movie ....]				Concert	Howard K. Smith

MONDAY
1962

	7:00	7:30	8:00	8:30	9:00	9:30	10:00	10:30
CBS	News	To Tell the Truth	I've Got a Secret	The Lucy Show	Danny Thomas	Andy Griffith	Loretta Young Show	Stump the Stars
NBC	Biography	[. It's a Man's World]		[. Saints and Sinners .]		The Price Is Right	[.. Telephone Hour .]	
ABC	Ann Sothern	[...... Cheyenne ......]		The Rifleman	[... Stony Burke ...]		[..... Ben Casey .....]	

TUESDAY
1962

	7:00	7:30	8:00	8:30	9:00	9:30	10:00	10:30
CBS	News	Marshal Dillon	Lloyd Bridges Show	[. Red Skelton Show .]		Jack Benny Show	[Garry Moore Show]	
NBC	The Story of . . .	[. . . . . . Laramie . . . . . .]		[. . . . . . Empire . . . . . .]		[. . . . . Dick Powell . . . .]		Chet Huntley
ABC	Phil Silvers	[. . . . . . Combat . . . . . .]		[. . . . Hawaiian Eye . . . .]		[. The Untouchables]		Here's Eddie

WEDNESDAY
1962

	7:00	7:30	8:00	8:30	9:00	9:30	10:00	10:30
CBS	News	[. . . CBS Reports . . .]		Dobie Gillis	The Beverly Hillbillies	Dick Van Dyke	[. . . . . . . Play . . . .]	
NBC	Death Valley Days	[. . . . . The Virginian . . . .]			[. . . . . Bob Hope . . . . .]		The Eleventh Hour	
ABC	The Rebel	[. . . Wagon Train . . .]		[. . Going My Way . .]		Our Man Higgins	[. . . . . Naked City . . . . .]	

THURSDAY
1962

	7:00	7:30	8:00	8:30	9:00	9:30	10:00	10:30
CBS	News	Mister Ed	[... Perry Mason ...]		[..... The Nurses ...]		[Alfred Hitchcock Hour]	
NBC	Ripcord	[... Wide Country ..]		[..... Dr. Kildare .....]		Hazel	[.. Andy Williams ..]	
ABC	Guestward Ho!	Ozzie and Harriet	Donna Reed Show	Leave It to Beaver	My Three Sons	McHale's Navy	[.. Alcoa Premiere ..]	

FRIDAY
1962

	7:00	7:30	8:00	8:30	9:00	9:30	10:00	10:30
CBS	Local	[...... Rawhide ......]		[...... Route 66 ......]		[.. Fair Exchange ..]	Eye Witness	
NBC	Local	[....... International Showtime ......]		[...... Hall of Fame ....]		[...... Jack Paar .....]		
ABC	Local	[. The Gallant Men .]		The Flintstones	I'm Dickens, He's Fenster	[... 77 Sunset Strip ..]		Local

SATURDAY 1962

	7:00	7:30	8:00	8:30	9:00	9:30	10:00	10:30
CBS	Local	[... Jackie Gleason ...]		[... The Defenders ..]		Have Gun Will Travel	[..... Gunsmoke .....]	
NBC	Local	[... Sam Benedict ..]		Joey Bishop	[............... Movie ....]			
ABC	Local	Roy Rogers and Dale Evans [.......]		Mr. Smith Goes to D.C.	[.. Lawrence Welk ..]		[.. Sporting Events .]	

SUNDAY 1963

	7:00	7:30	8:00	8:30	9:00	9:30	10:00	10:30
CBS	Lassie	My Favorite Martian [.	... Ed Sullivan Show .]		[...	Judy Garland ...]	Candid Camera	What's My Line?
NBC	Bill Dana Show	Walt Disney's Wonderful World [.......]		[...... Bonanza ......]		[............. Special ....]		
ABC	Film	Travels of Jaimie McPheeters [.....]		[......... Arrest and Trial ....]			Laughs for Sale	News

MONDAY 1963

	7:00	7:30	8:00	8:30	9:00	9:30	10:00	10:30
CBS	News	To Tell the Truth	I've Got a Secret	The Lucy Show	Danny Thomas	Andy Griffith	[East Side, West Side]	
NBC	News	[..............	Movie	..............]	Hollywood and the Stars		[Sing Along with Mitch]	
ABC	Have Gun Will Travel	[. The Outer Limits .]		[.............	Wagon Train	.............]	[... Breaking Point ..]	

TUESDAY 1963

	7:00	7:30	8:00	8:30	9:00	9:30	10:00	10:30
CBS	News	Marshal Dillon	[. Red Skelton Show]		Petticoat Junction	Jack Benny	[.... Garry Moore ...]	
NBC	News	[..... Mr. Novak .....]		Redigo	[Richard Boone Show]		[Andy Williams Show]	
ABC	Phil Silvers	[...... Combat ......]		McHale's Navy	[........ Greatest Show on Earth ....]		[... The Fugitive ...]	

WEDNESDAY
1963

	7:00	7:30	8:00	8:30	9:00	9:30	10:00	10:30
CBS	News	[..... Chronicle .....]		Glynis	The Beverly Hillbillies	Dick Van Dyke Show	[... Danny Kaye ....]	
NBC	News	[........... The Virginian ....]			[..... Espionage .....]		[The Eleventh Hour]	
ABC	The Rifleman	Adventures of Ozzie and Harriet	Patty Duke	The Price Is Right	[..... Ben Casey ....]		[...... Channing .....]	

THURSDAY
1963

	7:00	7:30	8:00	8:30	9:00	9:30	10:00	10:30
CBS	News	Password	[...... Rawhide ......]		[... Perry Mason ...]		[...... (Special) ......]	
NBC	News	[.. Temple Houston .]		[...... Dr. Kildare .....]		Hazel	[. Suspense Theatre .]	
ABC	I'm Dickens, He's Fenster	The Flintstones	Donna Reed Show	My Three Sons	[.. Jimmy Dean Show]		Sid Caesar	Battle Line

FRIDAY
1963

	7:00	7:30	8:00	8:30	9:00	9:30	10:00	10:30
CBS	News	[· · Great Adventure ·]		[...... Route 66 ......]		Twilight Zone	[...... (Special) ......]	
NBC	News	[...... International Showtime ......]		[... Bob Hope Show .]		Harry's Girls	[...... Jack Paar ......]	
ABC	Lawbreakers	[... 77 Sunset Strip ...]		[...... Burke's Law ....]		Farmer's Daughter	[... Sporting Events .]	

SATURDAY
1963

	7:00	7:30	8:00	8:30	9:00	9:30	10:00	10:30
CBS	Sea Hunt	[... Jackie Gleason ...]		Phil Silvers Show	[... The Defenders ..]		[...... Gunsmoke ......]	
NBC	Biography	[... The Lieutenant ...]		Joey Bishop	[...................... Movie ....]			
ABC	Death Valley Days	[... Hootenanny ....]		[Lawrence Welk Show]	[............ Jerry Lewis ....]			

SUNDAY 1964

	7:00	7:30	8:00	8:30	9:00	9:30	10:00	10:30
CBS	Lassie	My Favorite Martian	[.. Ed Sullivan Show ..]		My Living Doll	Joey Bishop	Candid Camera	What's My Line?
NBC	News	Walt Disney's Wonderful [...... World ......]		Bill Dana	[...... Bonanza ......]		[.... The Rogues ...]	
ABC	Film	[... Wagon Train ...]		Broadside	[................. Movie ....]			

MONDAY 1964

	7:00	7:30	8:00	8:30	9:00	9:30	10:00	10:30
CBS	News	To Tell the Truth	I've Got a Secret	Andy Griffith	The Lucy Show	Many Happy Returns	[. Slattery's People .]	
NBC	News	90 Bristol Court #1	90 Bristol Court #2	90 Bristol Court #3	[Andy Williams Show]		[Alfred Hitchcock Hour]	
ABC	The Rifleman	Voyage to the Bottom of [...... the Sea ......]		No Time for Sergeants	Wendy and Me	Bing Crosby	[..... Ben Casey ......]	

TUESDAY
1964

	7:00	7:30	8:00	8:30	9:00	9:30	10:00	10:30
CBS	News	Eye on New York	World War One	[. Red Skelton Show .]		Petticoat Junction	[Doctors and Nurses]	
NBC	News	[....	Mr. Novak ....]	[Man from U.N.C.L.E.]		That Was the Week that Was	[... News Special ...]	
ABC	Phil Silvers	[......	Combat ......]	McHale's Navy	The Tycoon	Peyton Place	[... The Fugitive ....]	

WEDNESDAY
1964

	7:00	7:30	8:00	8:30	9:00	9:30	10:00	10:30
CBS	News	Face the Nation	Stage 2	News	Dick Van Dyke	Cara Williams Show	[... Danny Kaye ....]	
NBC	News	[..........	The Virginian	.........]	[..........	Movie	]	
ABC	Car 54, Where Are You? (R)	Adventures of Ozzie and Harriet	Patty Duke	Shindig	Mickey	[... Burke's Law ....]	News	

THURSDAY 1964

	7:00	7:30	8:00	8:30	9:00	9:30	10:00	10:30
CBS	News	The Munsters	[... Perry Mason ...]		Eydie Gormé	(News)	[.. The Defenders ...]	
NBC	News	[... Daniel Boone ...]		[..... Dr. Kildare .....]		Hazel	[..... Perry Como ....]	
ABC	I'm Dickens, He's Fenster	The Flintstones	Donna Reed Show	My Three Sons	Bewitched	Peyton Place	[..... Jimmy Dean ....]	

FRIDAY 1964

	7:00	7:30	8:00	8:30	9:00	9:30	10:00	10:30
CBS	News	[..... Rawhide ......]		[.. The Entertainers .]		Gomer Pyle	[...... Reporter ......]	
NBC	News	[..... International Showtime ......]		[.. Bob Hope Show .]		Jack Benny	[...... Jack Paar ....]	
ABC	McKeever and the Colonel (R)	Jonny Quest	Farmer's Daughter	The Adams Family	Valentine's Day	[Twelve O'Clock High]		Have Gun Will Travel (R)

SATURDAY
1964

	7:00	7:30	8:00	8:30	9:00	9:30	10:00	10:30
CBS	News	[... Jackie Gleason ...]		Gilligan's Island	[.... Mr. Broadway ...]		[..... Gunsmoke .....]	
NBC	It's Academic	Flipper	Mr. Magoo	Kentucky Jones	[................. Movie ....]			
ABC	Laramie	[... Outer Limits ....]		[..... Lawrence Welk Show ....]			[. Hollywood Palace .]	Show Street

SUNDAY
1965

	7:00	7:30	8:00	8:30	9:00	9:30	10:00	10:30
CBS	Lassie	My Favorite Martian	[. Ed Sullivan Show .]		[..... Perry Mason .....]		Candid Camera	
NBC	Telephone Hour	Walt Disney's Wonderful World [......... World ....]		Branded	[..... Bonanza ......]		Wackiest Ship in the Army [........ Army ....]	
ABC	Voyage to the Bottom of the Sea [...... the Sea ......]		The F.B.I.	[..... The F.B.I. ....]	[................. Movie ....]			

MONDAY 1965

	7:00	7:30	8:00	8:30	9:00	9:30	10:00	10:30
CBS	News	To Tell the Truth	I've Got a Secret	The Lucy Show	Andy Griffith	Hazel	[.. Steve Lawrence .]	
NBC	News	Hullabaloo	John Forsythe Show	Dr. Kildare	[Andy Williams Show]		[. Run for Your Life .]	
ABC	Passport 7	[Twelve O'Clock High]		Legend of Jesse James	A Man Called Shenandoah	Farmer's Daughter	[..... Ben Casey .....]	

TUESDAY 1965

	7:00	7:30	8:00	8:30	9:00	9:30	10:00	10:30
CBS	News	[...... Rawhide ......]		[. Red Skelton Show .]		Petticoat Junction	[.... CBS Reports ...]	
NBC	News	My Mother the Car	Please Don't Eat the Daisies	Dr. Kildare	[................ Movies ....]			
ABC	Passport 7	[...... Combat ......]		McHale's Navy	F Troop	Peyton Place	[..... The Fugitive ...]	

WEDNESDAY
1965

	7:00	7:30	8:00	8:30	9:00	9:30	10:00	10:30
CBS	News	[... Lost in Space ....]		The Beverly Hillbillies	Green Acres	Dick Van Dyke Show	[.	Danny Kaye Show]
NBC	News	[..........	The Virginian ....]		[.....	Bob Hope .....]	[.........	I Spy ....]
ABC	Passport 7	Adventures of Ozzie and Harriet	Patty Duke	Gidget	[......	Big Valley .....]	Amos Burke, Secret Agent [........]	

THURSDAY
1965

	7:00	7:30	8:00	8:30	9:00	9:30	10:00	10:30 —
CBS	News	The Munsters	Gilligan's Island	My Three Sons	[...............		Movie	]
NBC	News	[... Daniel Boone ...]		[...... Laredo ......]		Mona Mc-Cluskey	[. Dean Martin Show]	
ABC	Passport 7	Shindig	Donna Reed Show	O.K. Crak-erby	Bewitched	Peyton Place	[The Long Hot Summer]	

FRIDAY 1965

	7:00	7:30	8:00	8:30	9:00	9:30	10:00	10:30
CBS	News	[.. Wild, Wild West .]		Hogan's Heroes	Gomer Pyle	Smothers Brothers	[...... Special ......]	
NBC	News	Camp Runa-muck	Hank	[....... Convoy ......]		Mr. Roberts	Man From [.... U.N.C.L.E. ....]	
ABC	Passport 7	The Flint-stones	Tammy	The Addams Family	Honey West	Peyton Place	Teenage Revolution [...... (Special) ......]	

SATURDAY 1965

	7:00	7:30	8:00	8:30	9:00	9:30	10:00	10:30
CBS	News	[.. Jackie Gleason ...]		[... Trials of O'Brien .]		The Loner	[..... Gunsmoke .....]	
NBC	It's Aca-demic	Flipper	I Dream of Jeannie	Get Smart	[................. Movies ....]			
ABC	ABC Scope	[....... Shindig ......]		[... Lawrence Welk Show]	[... Jimmy Durante ..]	News		

SUNDAY
1966

	7:00	7:30	8:00	8:30	9:00	9:30	10:00	10:30
CBS	Lassie	It's About Time	[. Ed Sullivan Show .]		[Garry Moore Show]		Candid Camera	What's My Line
NBC	Bell Telephone Hour/ Actuality Specials	Walt Disney's Wonderful [........ World ....]		Hey Landlord	[...... Bonanza ......]		[Andy Williams Show]	
ABC	Voyage to the Bottom of [....... the Sea ....]		[...... The F.B.I. ......]		[............. ABC Sunday Night Movie ....]			

MONDAY
1966

	7:00	7:30	8:00	8:30	9:00	9:30	10:00	10:30
CBS	Local	Gilligan's Island	Run Buddy Run	The Lucy Show	Andy Griffith	Family Affair	Jean Arthur Show	I've Got a Secret
NBC	Local	The Monkees	I Dream of Jeanie	Roger Miller Show	[...... Road West ......]		[. Run for Your Life .]	
ABC	Local	[...... Iron Horse ......]		Rat Patrol	Felony Squad	Peyton Place	[...... Big Valley ......]	

TUESDAY
1966

	7:00	7:30	8:00	8:30	9:00	9:30	10:00	10:30
CBS	Local	[...... Daktari ......]		[. Red Skelton Hour .]		Petticoat Junction	[. CBS News Hour .]	
NBC	Local	[Girl from U.N.C.L.E.]		Occaisonal Wife	[........... NBC Tuesday Night Movie ....]			
ABC	Local	[...... Combat ......]		The Roun-ders	Pruits of Southhamp-ton	Love on a Rooftop	[.... The Fugitive ....]	

WEDNESDAY
1966

	7:00	7:30	8:00	8:30	9:00	9:30	10:00	10:30
CBS	Local	[... Lost is Space ...]		The Beverly Hillbillies	Green Acres	Gomer Pyle, U.S.M.C.	[. Danny Kaye Show]	
NBC	Local	[........... The Virginian ....]			Bob Hope Presents The [.. Chrysler Theatre ..]		[........... I Spy ....]	
ABC	Local	Batman	[.... The Monroes ....]		Man Who Never Was	Peyton Place	[.. ABC Stage '67 ..]	

THURSDAY
1966

	7:00	7:30	8:00	8:30	9:00	9:30	10:00	10:30
CBS	Local	[...... Jericho ......]		My Three Sons	[............ CBS Thursday Night Movie ....]			
NBC	Local	[... Daniel Boone ...]		[...... Star Trek ......]		The Hero	[. Dean Martin Show]	
ABC	Local	Batman	F Troop	Tammy Grimes Show	Bewitched	That Girl	[...... Hawk ......]	

FRIDAY
1966

	7:00	7:30	8:00	8:30	9:00	9:30	10:00	10:30
CBS	Local	[.. Wild Wild West ..]		Hogan's Heros	[............ CBS Friday Night Movie ....]			
NBC	Local	[...... Tarzan ......]		[Man From U.N.C.L.E.]		T.H.E. Cat	[...... Laredo ......]	
ABC	Local	Green Hornet	[... Time Tunnel ...]		[. Milton Berle Show]		[Twelve O'Clock High]	

SATURDAY 1966

	7:00	7:30	8:00	8:30	9:00	9:30	10:00	10:30
CBS	Local	[Jackie Gleason Show]		Pistols 'N' Petticoats	[Mission Impossible]		[..... Gunsmoke .....]	
NBC	Local	Flipper	Please Don't Eat The Daisies	Get Smart	[........... NBC Saturday Night Movie ....]			
ABC	Local	[...... Shane ....]		[Lawrence Welk Show]		[. Hollywood Palace .]		ABC Scope

SUNDAY 1967

	7:00	7:30	8:00	8:30	9:00	9:30	10:00	10:30
CBS	Lassie	Gentle Ben	[. Ed Sullivan Show .]		[. Smothers Brothers]		[Mission: Impossible]	
NBC	Sports	Walt Disney's Wonderful World [........]		The Mothers in-Law	[...... Bonanza ......]		[.. High Chaparral ...]	
ABC	Voyage to the Bottom of the Sea [......]		[..... The F.B.I. .....]		[...................... Movie ....]			

MONDAY 1967

	7:00	7:30	8:00	8:30	9:00	9:30	10:00	10:30
CBS	News	[.... Gunsmoke ....]		The Lucy Show	Andy Griffith	Family Affair	[Carol Burnett Show]	
NBC	News	The Monkeys	[.... U.N.C.L.E. ....] The Man from		[Danny Thomas Hour]		[........ I Spy ....]	
ABC	Film	[. Cowboy in Africa .]		[........ Special ....]		Peyton Place	[........ Special ....]	

TUESDAY 1967

	7:00	7:30	8:00	8:30	9:00	9:30	10:00	10:30
CBS	News	[........ Daktari ....]		[. Red Skelton Show .]		Good Morning, World	[... News Special ...]	
NBC	News	I Dream of Jeannie	[. Jerry Lewis Show .]		[.......... Movie ....]			
ABC	Film	[. Garrison's Gorillas .]		[... The Invaders ....]		[........ Circle Theatre ....]		

WEDNESDAY
1967

	7:00	7:30	8:00	8:30	9:00	9:30	10:00	10:30
CBS	News	[..... Lost in Space .....]		The Beverly Hillbillies	Green Acres	He & She	Dundee and the Culhane .....]	
NBC	News	[.......... The Virginian ....]			[..... Music Hall .....]		[..... Run for Your Life .]	
ABC	Film	[.......... Movie ....]					[..... Special ......]	

THURSDAY
1967

	7:00	7:30	8:00	8:30	9:00	9:30	10:00	10:30
CBS	News	Special	[..... Special .....]		[.......... Movie ....]			
NBC	News	[..... Daniel Boone ...]		[..... Ironside ......]		Dragnet	[. Dean Martin Show]	
ABC	Film	Batman	Flying Nun	Bewitched	That Girl	Peyton Place	Good Company	What Is ... Really Like?

FRIDAY
1967

	7:00	7:30	8:00	8:30	9:00	9:30	10:00	10:30
CBS	News	[.. Wild, Wild West .]		Gomer Pyle	[................ Movie ....]			
NBC	News	[....... Tarzan ....]		[...... Star Trek ......]		Accidental Family	[..... News Special .....]	
ABC	Film	[........ Film ....]		[........ Hondo ....]		Guns of Will Sonnett	[.. John Davidson ..]	

SATURDAY
1967

	7:00	7:30	8:00	8:30	9:00	9:30	10:00	10:30
CBS	News	[... Jackie Gleason ..]		My Three Sons	Hogan's Heroes	Petticoat Junction	[....... Mannix ....]	
NBC	It's Academic	[........ Maya ....]		Get Smart	[................ Movie ....]			
ABC	Dating Game	The Rifleman	Newlywed Game	[Lawrence Welk Show]		[..... Iron Horse .....]		News

SUNDAY 1968

	7:00	7:30	8:00	8:30	9:00	9:30	10:00	10:30
CBS	Lassie	Gentle Ben	[. Ed Sullivan Show .]		[..... Pat Paulsen ...]		[Mission: Impossible]	
NBC	New Adventures of Huckleberry Finn	Walt Disney's Wonderful [........ World ....]		The Mothers-in-Law	[..... Bonanza ......]		[.... Phyllis Diller ....]	
ABC	[. Land of the Giants]		[..... The F.B.I. .....]		[.................. Movie ....]			

MONDAY 1968

	7:00	7:30	8:00	8:30	9:00	9:30	10:00	10:30
CBS	News	[..... Gunsmoke .....]		Here's Lucy	Mayberry, R.F.D.	Family Affair	[Carol Burnett Show]	
NBC	News	Special	Rowan and Martin's [...... Laugh-In ......]		[................. Movie ....]			
ABC	Local	[.... The Avengers ..]		Peyton Place	[....... Special ......]		[...... Big Valley .....]	

TUESDAY
1968

	7:00	7:30	8:00	8:30	9:00	9:30	10:00	10:30
CBS	News	[...... Lancer ......]		[The Red Skelton Show]		Doris Day	[...... 60 Minutes .....]	
NBC	News	[. Jerry Lewis Show .]		Julia	[.................. Movie ....]			
ABC	Sports	[... The Mod Squad ..]		[... It Takes a Thief ..]		N.Y.P.D.	[...... That's Life .....]	

WEDNESDAY
1968

	7:00	7:30	8:00	8:30	9:00	9:30	10:00	10:30
CBS	News	[National Geographic Special ......]		The Good Guys	Beverly Hillbillies	Green Acres	[. Jonathan Winters .]	
NBC	News	[.......... The Virginian ....]		[. Kraft Music Hall .]		[.... Bing Crosby ...]		
ABC	News	[Here Come the Brides]		Peyton Place	[...... Special ......]		[...... Special ......]	

THURSDAY
1968

	7:00	7:30	8:00	8:30	9:00	9:30	10:00	10:30
CBS	News	Special	[...... Special ......]		[...... Movie ......]			
NBC	News	[... Daniel Boone ...]		[...... Ironside ......]		Dragnet	[. Dean Martin Show]	
ABC	News	Ugliest Girl in Town	Flying Nun	Bewitched	That Girl	Journey to the Unknown		Special

FRIDAY
1968

	7:00	7:30	8:00	8:30	9:00	9:30	10:00	10:30
CBS	News	[.. Wild, Wild West .]		Gomer Pyle	[...... Movie ......]			
NBC	News	[... High Chaparral ..]		[...... The Name of the Game ......]			[...... Star Trek ......]	
ABC	News	Operation Entertainment	Felony Squad		[...... Special ......]		Judd for the Defense	

SATURDAY
1968

	7:00	7:30	8:00	8:30	9:00	9:30	10:00	10:30
CBS	News	[... Jackie Gleason ...]		My Three Sons	Hogan's Heroes	Petticoat Junction	[...... Mannix ......]	
NBC	News	Adam-12	Get Smart	The Ghost and Mrs. Muir	[.............. Movie ....]			
ABC	News	Dating Game	Newlywed Game	[Lawrence Welk Show]		[. Hollywood Palace .]		Special

SUNDAY
1969

	7:00	7:30	8:00	8:30	9:00	9:30	10:00	10:30
CBS	Lassie	To Rome With Love	[. Ed Sullivan Show .]		[Leslie Uggams Show]		[Mission: Impossible]	
NBC	Wild Kingdom	Walt Disney's Wonderful [... World of Color ...]		Bill Cosby Show	[...... Bonanza ......]		[... The Bold Ones ...]	
ABC	[. Land of the Giants]		[...... The F.B.I. ......]		[............ ABC Sunday Night Movie ....]			

MONDAY 1969

	7:00	7:30	8:00	8:30	9:00	9:30	10:00	10:30
CBS	News	[..... Gunsmoke .....]		Here's Lucy	Mayberry, R.F.D.	Doris Day Show	[Carol Burnett Show]	
NBC	News	My World and Welcome to It	Rowan and Martin's [...... Laugh-In ......]		[.......... NBC Monday Night Movie ....]			
ABC	News	[.... Music Scene ...]		The New People	[.... The Survivors ...]		[Love, American Style]	

TUESDAY 1969

	7:00	7:30	8:00	8:30	9:00	9:30	10:00	10:30
CBS	News	[....... Lancer ....]		[. Red Skelton Hour .]		The Governor and J.J.	[..... 60 Minutes .....]	
NBC	News	I Dream of Jeannie	Debbie Reynolds Show	Julia	[.......... NBC Tuesday Night Movie ....]			
ABC	News	[.... Mod Squad .....]		[.......... Movie of the Week ....]		Marcus Welby, M.D.		

WEDNESDAY
1969

	7:00	7:30	8:00	8:30	9:00	9:30	10:00	10:30
CBS	News	Glen Cambell Good Time Hour [........]		Beverly Hillbillies	[... Medical Center ..]		[... Hawaii Five-O ...]	
NBC	News	[......... The Virginian ....]			[. Kraft Music Hall .]		[Then Came Bronson]	
ABC	News	Flying Nun	Courtship of Eddie's Father	Room 222	[.......... ABC Wednesday Night Movie ....]			

THURSDAY
1969

	7:00	7:30	8:00	8:30	9:00	9:30	10:00	10:30
CBS	News	Family Af-fair	[. Jim Nabors Hour .]		[........... CBS Thursday Night Movie ....]			
NBC	News	[... Daniel Boone ....]		[...... Ironside ......]		Dragnet	[. Dean Martin Show]	
ABC	News	The Ghost and Mrs. Muir	That Girl	Bewitched	[. This Is Tom Jones]		[.. It Takes a Thief ..]	

FRIDAY 1969

	7:00	7:30	8:00	8:30	9:00	9:30	10:00	10:30
CBS	News	Get Smart	The Good Guys	Hogan's Heroes	[············· CBS Friday Night Movie ···········]			
NBC	News	[··· High Chaparral ··]	[······· The Name of The Game ······]				[··· Bracken's World ·]	
ABC	News	Let's Make a Deal	The Brady Bunch	Mr. Deeds Goes to Town	[Here Come the Brides]		Jimmy Durante Presents the Lennon Sisters ·	

SATURDAY 1969

	7:00	7:30	8:00	8:30	9:00	9:30	10:00	10:30
CBS	News	[Jackie Gleason Show]	My Three Sons	Green Acres	Petticoat Junction	[······· Mannix ······]		
NBC	News	[Andy Williams Show]	Adam-12	[··········· NBC Saturday Night Movie ··········]				
ABC	News	Dating Game	Newlywed Game	[Lawrence Welk Show]	[·· Hollywood Palace ·]		One Man Show	

SUNDAY 1970

	7:00	7:30	8:00	8:30	9:00	9:30	10:00	10:30
CBS	Lassie	Hogan's Heroes	Ed Sullivan Show [........]		Glen Cambell Goodtime Hour [........]		Tim Conway Comedy Hour [........]	
NBC	Wild Kingdom	Walt Disney (Wonderful World of) [......]		Bill Cosby Show	Bonanza [......]		The Bold Ones [...]	
ABC		[... Young Rebels ...]		The F.B.I. [...]	ABC Sunday Night Movie [.........]			

MONDAY 1970

	7:00	7:30	8:00	8:30	9:00	9:30	10:00	10:30
CBS	News	[.... Gunsmoke .....]		Here's Lucy	Mayberry, R.F.D.	Doris Day Show	Carol Burnett Show [ ]	
NBC	News	Red Skelton Show	Rowan and Martin's Laugh-in [......]		NBC Monday Night Movie [.........]			
ABC	News	The Young Lawyers		The Silent Force	Sporting Events [.........]			

TUESDAY 1970

	7:00	7:30	8:00	8:30	9:00	9:30	10:00	10:30
CBS	News	Beverly Hillbillies	Green Acres	[..... Hee-Haw	]	To Rome with Love	[..... 60 Minutes .....]	
NBC	News	[. Don Knotts Show .]	Julia	[.......... NBC Tuesday Night Movie ....]				
ABC	News	[... The Mod Squad ..]	[........	Movie of the Week ....]	[Marcus Welby, M.D.]			

WEDNESDAY 1970

	7:00	7:30	8:00	8:30	9:00	9:30	10:00	10:30
CBS	News	[Storefront Lawyers .]	The Governer and J.J.	[... Medical Center ..]	[... Hawaii Five-O ..]			
NBC	News	[........ Men from Shiloh ....]	[. Kraft Music Hall .]	[... Four-in-One ...]				
ABC	News	Courtship of Eddie's Father	Danny Thomas: Make Room for Grand-daddy	Room 222	[Johnny Cash Show]	[..... Dan August ....]		

THURSDAY
1970

	7:00	7:30	8:00	8:30	9:00	9:30	10:00	10:30
CBS	News	Family Affair	[. Jim Nabors Hour .]	[............	CBS Thursday Night Movie ....]			
NBC	News	[. Flip Wilson Show .]	[......]	[. Ironside ......]	[. Nancy	[. Dean Martin Show]		
ABC	News	[.... Matt Lincoln ....]	Bewitched	Barefoot in the Park	Odd Couple	[.... The Immortal ...]		

FRIDAY
1970

	7:00	7:30	8:00	8:30	9:00	9:30	10:00	10:30
CBS	News	[.... The Interns ...]	The Headmaster	[.............	CBS Friday Night Movie ....]			
NBC	News	[.. High Chaparral ..]	[........]	Name of the Game ....]	[.. Bracken's World .]			
ABC	News	The Brady Bunch	Nanny and the Professor	Partridge Family	That Girl	Love, American Style	[. This Is Tom Jones]	

SATURDAY
1970

	7:00	7:30	8:00	8:30	9:00	9:30	10:00	10:30
CBS	News	[Mission Impossible]		My Three Sons	Arnie	Mary Tyler Moore Show	[Mannix	]
NBC	News	[Andy Williams Show]		Adam-12	[..........	NBC Saturday Night Movie		..........]
ABC	News	Let's Make a Deal	Newlywed Game	[Lawrence Welk Show]		The Most [.... Deadly Game ....]		Nashville Now

SUNDAY
1971

	7:00	7:30	8:00	8:30	9:00	9:30	10:00	10:30
CBS	News	Aesop's Fables	[.. Ed Sullivan Show .]		[..	Cade's County ..]		David Frost
NBC	Wild Kingdom	[....... Wonderful World of Disney ....]		Jimmy Stewart Show	[......	Bonanza ......]	[......	Bold Ones ....]
ABC	[...... Local ......]		[..... The F.B.I. .....]		[............]		ABC Sunday Night Movie	..........]

239

MONDAY 1971

	7:00	7:30	8:00	8:30	9:00	9:30	10:00	10:30
CBS	News	Johnny Mann's Stand Up and Cheer	[.... Gunsmoke .....]		Here's Lucy	Doris Day Show	My Three Sons	Arnie
NBC	News	Dr. Simon Locke	Rowan and Martin's Laugh-In [.......]		[............. NBC Monday Night Movie ....]			
ABC	News	Story Theatre	Nanny and the Professor	In the Game	[............ Sporting Events ....]			

TUESDAY 1971

	7:00	7:30	8:00	8:30	9:00	9:30	10:00	10:30
CBS	News	Glen Campbell Goodtime Hour [.......]		[... Hawaii Five-O ..]		[60 Minutes/Cannon]		The Gold-diggers
NBC	News	[..... Ironside ......]			Sarge ......]	[.. The Funny Side ..]		
ABC	News	[.. The Mod Squad ..]		[.......... Movie of the Week ....]			[Marcus Welby, M.D]	

WEDNESDAY 1971

	7:00	7:30	8:00	8:30	9:00	9:30	10:00	10:30
CBS	News	Doctor in the House	[Carol Burnett Show]		[.. Medical Center ..]		[...... Mannix ......]	
NBC	News	Primus	Adam-12	[...... NBC Mystery Movie ......]			[.... Night Gallery ....]	
ABC	News	Safari to Adventure	Bewitched	Courtship of Eddie's Father	The Smith Family	Shirley's World	[The Man and the City]	

THURSDAY 1971

	7:00	7:30	8:00	8:30	9:00	9:30	10:00	10:30
CBS	News	Kenny Rogers and the First Edition	[...... Bearcats ......]		[...... CBS Thursday Night Movie ....]			
NBC	News	Lassie	[.. Flip Wilson Show .]		Nichols [.... (James Garner) ....]		[.. Dean Martin Show]	
ABC	News	This Is Your Life	[.. Alias Smith and Jones]		[..... Longstreet .....]		Owen Marshall: [.. Counselor at Law . .]	

FRIDAY
1971

	7:00	7:30	8:00	8:30	9:00	9:30	10:00	10:30
CBS	News	Circus	Chicago Teddy Bears	[O'Hara, U.S. Treasury]		[......	New CBS Friday Movie	......]
NBC	News	Hollywood Squares	The D.A.	[............	NBC World Premiere Movie	............]		Monty Nash
ABC	News	Let's Make a Deal	The Brady Bunch	Partridge Family	Room 222	The Odd Couple	[Love, American Style]	

SATURDAY
1971

	7:00	7:30	8:00	8:30	9:00	9:30	10:00	10:30
CBS	News	Jerry Visits	All in the Family	Funny Face	New Dick Van Dyke Show	Mary Tyler Moore Show	[Mission: Impossible]	
NBC	[...	News Special ...]	The Part-ners	The Good Life	NBC Saturday Night [........ Movie ......]		[........	News ......]
ABC	News	Anything You Can Do	[............	ABC Movie of the Weekend	............]		[... The Persuaders ..]	

SUNDAY 1972

	7:00	7:30	8:00	8:30	9:00	9:30	10:00	10:30
CBS	News	Anna and the King	M*A*S*H	Sandy Duncan Show	New Dick Van Dyke Show	[...... Mannix ......]		The Protectors
NBC	Wild Kingdom	Wonderful World of Walt Disney [.......]		[... NBC Sunday Mystery Movie ...]			Night Gallery	News
ABC	[... News (Special) ...]		[...... The FBI ......]		[........ ABC Sunday Night Movie ....]			

MONDAY 1972

	7:00	7:30	8:00	8:30	9:00	9:30	10:00	10:30
CBS	News	Johnny Mann's Stand Up and Cheer	[.... Gunsmoke ....]		Here's Lucy	Doris Day Show	[New Bill Cosby Show]	
NBC	News	The Mouse Factory	Rowan and Martin's Laugh-In [......]		[........ Movie ....]			
ABC	News	World of Survival	[.... The Rookies ....]		[........ Sporting Events ....]			

TUESDAY
1972

	7:00	7:30	8:00	8:30	9:00	9:30	10:00	10:30
CBS	News	I've Got a Secret	Maude	[···· Hawaii Five-O ···]		[············· (Special) ·············]		
NBC	News	Wait Till Your Father Gets Home	[······ Bonanza ······]		[··· The Bold Ones ··]		[···· News Special ···]	
ABC	News	[Safari to Adventure ··]	[············· Movie ·············]				[Marcus Welby, M.D.]	

WEDNESDAY
1972

	7:00	7:30	8:00	8:30	9:00	9:30	10:00	10:30
CBS	News	The Gold-diggers	[Carol Burnett Show]		[·· Medical Center ··]		[········ Cannon ······]	
NBC	News	Police Surgeon	Adam-12	[············· Movie ·············]			[········ Search ·······]	
ABC	News	Parent Game	Paul Lynde	[············· Movie ·············]			[Julie Andrews Show]	

THURSDAY
1972

	7:00	7:30	8:00	8:30	9:00	9:30	10:00	10:30
CBS	News	Young Dr. Kildare	[.... The Waltons ....]		[.......................... Movie ....]			
NBC	News	Hollywood Squares	[. Flip Wilson Show .]		[....... Ironside ......]		[.... Dean Martin Show]	
ABC	News	Adventures of Black Beauty	[... The Mod Squad ...]		[...... The Men ......]		[... Owen Marshall: Counselor at Law .]	

FRIDAY
1972

	7:00	7:30	8:00	8:30	9:00	9:30	10:00	10:30
CBS	News	Circus	Sonny and Cher Comedy [....... Hour ....]		[.......................... Movie ....]			
NBC	News	The Adventurer	Sandford and Son	The Little People	[.... Ghost Story ...]		[....... Banyon ......]	
ABC	News	Let's Make a Deal	The Brady Bunch	Partridge Family	Room 222	The Odd Couple	[Love, American Style]	

SATURDAY
1972

	7:00	7:30	8:00	8:30	9:00	9:30	10:00	10:30
CBS	[........	UFO ....]	All in the Family	Bridget Loves Bernie	Mary Tyler Moore Show	Bob Newhart Show	[Mission: Impossible]	
NBC	News	The New Price Is Right	[.................		.... Movie		.................]	
ABC	News	Explorers	[Aliasa Smith and Jones]		Streets of San Francisco [........]		[... The Sixth Sense .]	

SUNDAY
1973

	7:00	7:30	8:00	8:30	9:00	9:30	10:00	10:30
CBS	News	New Adventures of Perry Mason [........]		[........	Mannix ....]	[...	Barnaby Jones ..]	The Protectors
NBC	Wild Kingdom	Wonderful World of Disney [........]		[........	NBC Sunday Mystery Movie		]	News
ABC	Ozzie's Girls	[........	The F.B.I. ......]	[............	ABC Sunday Night Movie		]	Evil Touch

MONDAY
1973

	7:00	7:30	8:00	8:30	9:00	9:30	10:00	10:30
CBS	News	Johnny Man's Stand Up and Cheer	[.... Gunsmoke .....]		Here's Lucy	New Dick Van Dyke Show	[... Medical Center ..]	
NBC	News	Hollywood Squares	Lotsa Luck	Diana	[............ NBC Monday Night Movie ....]			
ABC	News	World of Survival	[.... The Rookies ...]		[.............. Sporting Events ....]			

TUESDAY
1973

	7:00	7:30	8:00	8:30	9:00	9:30	10:00	10:30
CBS	News	New Treasure Hunt	Maude	[... Hawaii Five-O ...]		[.............. Shaft ....]		
NBC	News	Safari to Adventure	[....... Chase ......]		[.... The Magician ...]		[..... Police Story ....]	
ABC	News	Temperatures Rising	[.............. Tuesday Movie of the Week ....]				[Marcus Welby, M.D.]	

WEDNESDAY
1973

	7:00	7:30	8:00	8:30	9:00	9:30	10:00	10:30
CBS	News	Orson Welles	Sonny and Cher Comedy [........ Hour ....]		Cannon ......]	[........	[........	Kojak ....]
NBC	News	The Price Is Right	Adam-12	[....	NBC Wednesday Mystery Movie .]	[.....	Love Story .....]	
ABC	News	Strange Places	Bob and Carol and Ted and Alice	[...	Wednesday Movie of the Week ...]		Owen Marshall: [.. Counselor at Law .]	

THURSDAY
1973

	7:00	7:30	8:00	8:30	9:00	9:30	10:00	10:30
CBS	News	Wacky World of Jonathan Winters	[....	The Waltons ...]	[............	CBS Thursday Night Movie ....]		
NBC	News	Hollywood Squares	[.. Flip Wilson Show .]		[......	Ironside ......]	[...	NBC Follies ....]
ABC	News	[.... Animal World ..] Toma			[......	Kung Fu ......]	Streets of San [...... Francisco ......]	

FRIDAY 1973

	7:00	7:30	8:00	8:30	9:00	9:30	10:00	10:30
CBS	News	Dusty's Trail	Calucci's Department	Roll Out	[············ CBS Friday Night Movie ············]			
NBC	News	Police Surgeon	Sanford and Son	Girl with Something Extra	Needles and Pins	Brian Keith Show	[· Dean Martin Show]	
ABC	News	Let's Make a Deal	The Brady Bunch	The Odd Couple	Room 222	Adam's Rib	[Love, American Style]	

SATURDAY 1973

	7:00	7:30	8:00	8:30	9:00	9:30	10:00	10:30
CBS	News	News Special	All in the Family	M*A*S*H	Mary Tyler Moore Show	Bob Newhart Show	[Carol Burnett Show]	
NBC	[······ Starlost ······]		[····· Emergency ·····]		[···· NBC Saturday Night Movie ····]			
ABC	[······ People, Places and ······· Things ·······]		Partridge Family	[······· ABC Suspense Movie ·······]			[··· Doc Elliot/Griff ··]	

SUNDAY
1974

	7:00	7:30	8:00	8:30	9:00	9:30	10:00	10:30
CBS	News	[… Apple's Way …]		[…… Kojak ……]		[…… Manix ……]		The Protectors (R)
NBC	Wild Kingdom	Wonderful World of Disney ……]	[	[…… Columbo ……]		[… NBC Sunday Mystery Movie …]		
ABC	Celebrity Sweepstakes	Let's Make a Deal	[… Sonny Comedy Revue]		[…………… ABC Sunday Night Movie ……………]			

MONDAY
1974

	7:00	7:30	8:00	8:30	9:00	9:30	10:00	10:30
CBS	News	[…… Gunsmoke ……]		Maude	Rhoda	[… Medical Center ..]		
NBC	News	Hollywood Squares	[… Born Free ……]	[…………… NBC Monday Night Movie ……………]				
ABC	News	World of Survival	[… The Rookies …]	[…………… Sporting Events ……………]				

TUESDAY
1974

	7:00	7:30	8:00	8:30	9:00	9:30	10:00	10:30
CBS	News	New Treasure Hunt	Good Times	M*A*S*H	[… Hawaii Five-O …]		[… Barnaby Jones ..]	
NBC	News	Jeopardy	Adam-12	[… NBC World Premiere Movie ……]			[…… Police Story ….]	
ABC	News	Wild, Wild World of Animals	Happy Days	[… Tuesday Movie of the Week ….]			[Marcus Welby, M.D.]	

WEDNESDAY
1974

	7:00	7:30	8:00	8:30	9:00	9:30	10:00	10:30
CBS	News	Last of the Wild	[Sons and Daughters]		[……. Cannon ……]		[… The Manhunter ..]	
NBC	News	Name that Tune	[…… Little House on the Prairie …….]		[… Lucas Tanner ..]		[…… Petrocelli …..]	
ABC	News	Rainbow Sundae	That's My Mama	[Wednesday TV Movie of the Week .]			[. Get Christie Love!]	

THURSDAY
1974

	7:00	7:30	8:00	8:30	9:00	9:30	10:00	10:30
CBS	News	The $25,000 Pyramid	[... The Waltons ...]		[............ CBS Thursday Night Movie ....]			
NBC	News	Hollywood Squares	[...... Sierra ......]		[...... Ironside ......]		[...... Movin' On ......]	
ABC	News	Strange Places	The Odd Couple	Paper Moon	Streets of San [...... Francisco ......]		[...... Harry O ......]	

FRIDAY
1974

	7:00	7:30	8:00	8:30	9:00	9:30	10:00	10:30
CBS	News	Masquerade Party	[... Planet of the Apes]		[............ CBS Friday Night Movie ....]			
NBC	News	Safari to Ad-venture	Sanford and Son	Chico and the Man	[The Rockford Files]		[... Police Woman ...]	
ABC	News	Let's Make a Deal	[...... Kodiak ......]		[Six Million Dollar Man]		The Kolchak: The Night [...... Stalker ......]	

SATURDAY
1974

	7:00	7:30	8:00	8:30	9:00	9:30	10:00	10:30
CBS	News	New Candid Camera	All in the Family	Friends and Lovers	Mary Tyler Moore Show	Bob New- hart Show	[Carol Burnett Show]	
NBC	To Tell the Truth	The Price Is Right	[..... Emergency ......]		[........... NBC Saturday Night Movie ....]			
ABC	People, Places and Things	Animal World	[.. The New Land ...]		[...... Kung Fu ......]		[....... Nakia ....]	

SUNDAY
1975

	7:00	7:30	8:00	8:30	9:00	9:30	10:00	10:30
CBS	[. Three for the Road]		[........ Cher ....]		[....... Kojak ....]		[....... Bronk ....]	
NBC	Wonderful World of [...... Disney ......]		[The Family Holvak]		[........... NBC Sunday Mystery Movie ....]			
ABC	Swiss Family [...... Robinson ......]		[Six Million Dollar Man]		[........... ABC Sunday Night Movie ....]			

MONDAY 1975

	7:00	7:30	8:00	8:30	9:00	9:30	10:00	10:30
CBS	News	Bobby Vinton	Rhoda	Phyllis	All in the Family	Maude	[... Medical Center ...]	
NBC	News	Hollywood Squares	[... Invisible Man ...]		[............ NBC Monday Night Movie ....]			
ABC	News	Sacajawea	[... Barbary Coast ..]		[................ Sporting Events ....]			

TUESDAY 1975

	7:00	7:30	8:00	8:30	9:00	9:30	10:00	10:30
CBS	News	New Treasure Hunt	Good Times	Joe and Sons	[...... Switch ......]		[... Beacon Hill ...]	
NBC	News	Wild Kingdom	[... Movin' On .....]		[... Police Story ...]		[... Joe Forrester ...]	
ABC	News	Let's Make a Deal	Happy Days	Welcome Back, Kotter	[... The Rookies ...]		[... Marcus Welby, M.D.]	

254

WEDNESDAY 1975

	7:00	7:30	8:00	8:30	9:00	9:30	10:00	10:30
CBS	News	Last of the Wild	[Tony Orlando and Dawn]		[Cannon]		[Kate McShane]	
NBC	News	Name that Tune	[Little House on the Prairie]		[Doctors Hospital]		[Petrocelli]	
ABC	News	Match Game PM	When Things Were Rotten	That's My Mama	[Baretta]		[Starsky and Hutch]	

THURSDAY 1975

	7:00	7:30	8:00	8:30	9:00	9:30	10:00	10:30
CBS	News	The $25,000 Pyramid	[The Waltons]		[CBS Thursday Night Movie]			
NBC	News	Hollywood Squares	The Montefuscos	Fay	[Ellery Queen]		[Medical Story]	
ABC	News	Wild, Wild World of Animals	Barney Miller	On the Rocks	[Streets of San Francisco]		[Harry O]	

FRIDAY
1975

	7:00	7:30	8:00	8:30	9:00	9:30	10:00	10:30
CBS	News	New Candid Camera	Big Eddie	M*A*S*H	[.. Hawaii Five-O ..]	[.. Barnaby Jones ..]		
NBC	News	Don Adams' Screen Test	Sanford and Son	Chico and the Man	[.. Rockford Files ..]	[.... Police Woman ..]		
ABC	News	High Rollers	[..... Mobile One ....]	[............. ABC Friday Night Movie ....]				

SATURDAY
1975

	7:00	7:30	8:00	8:30	9:00	9:30	10:00	10:30
CBS	News	The People	The Jeffersons	Doc	Mary Tyler Moore Show	Bob Newhart Show	[Carol Burnett Show]	
NBC	Film	The Price Is Right	[..... Emergency .....]	[............. NBC Saturday Night Movie ....]				
ABC	News	Let's Make a Deal	Saturday Night Live With ... Howard Cosell ...]	[...... S.W.A.T. ......]	[..... Matt Helm .....]			

SUNDAY 1976

	7:00	7:30	8:00	8:30	9:00	9:30	10:00	10:30
CBS	[..... 60 Minutes .....]		[..... Sonny and Cher Comedy Hour ....]		[....... Kojak ....]		[..... Delvecchio .....]	
NBC	Wonderful World of Disney [........]		[.... NBC Sunday Mystery Movie ...]		[...... Big Event ......]			
ABC	[........ Cos ....]		[Six Million Dollar Man]		[........ ABC Sunday Night Movie ....]			

MONDAY 1976

	7:00	7:30	8:00	8:30	9:00	9:30	10:00	10:30
CBS	[........ Local ....]		Rhoda	Phyllis	Maude	All's Fair	[... Executive Suite ...]	
NBC	[........ Local ....]		Little House on the Prairie [........]		[........ NBC Monday Night Movie ....]			
ABC	[........ Local ....]		The Captain and Tennille [........]		[........ Sporting Events ....]			

256

TUESDAY
1976

	7:00	7:30	8:00	8:30	9:00	9:30	10:00	10:30
CBS	[⋯⋯⋯ Local ⋯⋯⋯]		[Tony Orlando and Dawn / ⋯ Rainbow Hour ⋯]		M*A*S*H	One Day at a Time	[⋯⋯⋯ Switch ⋯⋯⋯]	
NBC	[⋯⋯⋯ Local ⋯⋯⋯]		[⋯ Baa Baa Black Sheep]		[⋯ Police Woman ⋯]		[⋯ Police Story ⋯]	
ABC	[⋯⋯⋯ Local ⋯⋯⋯]		Happy Days	Laverne and Shirley	[Rich Man, Poor Man]		[⋯⋯⋯ Family ⋯⋯⋯]	

WEDNESDAY
1976

	7:00	7:30	8:00	8:30	9:00	9:30	10:00	10:30
CBS	[⋯⋯⋯ Local ⋯⋯⋯]		Good Times	Ball Four	All in the Family	Alice	[⋯ Blue Knight ⋯]	
NBC	[⋯⋯⋯ Local ⋯⋯⋯]		The Practice	[⋯⋯⋯ NBC Movie of the Week ⋯⋯⋯]			[⋯ The Quest ⋯]	
ABC	[⋯⋯⋯ Local ⋯⋯⋯]		[⋯ Bionic Woman ⋯]		[⋯⋯⋯ Baretta ⋯⋯⋯]		[⋯ Charlie's Angels ⋯]	

THURSDAY 1976

	7:00	7:30	8:00	8:30	9:00	9:30	10:00	10:30
CBS	[......	Local ......]	[...... The Waltons ...]		[... Hawaii Five-O ...]		[... Barnaby Jones ...]	
NBC	[......	Local ......]	[... Gemini Man ...]		[.. NBC Best Sellers .]		[...... Van Dyke and Company ......]	
ABC	[......	Local ......]	Welcome Back, Kotter	Barney Miller	Tony Randall Show	Nancy Walker Show	[...... Streets of San Francisco ......]	

FRIDAY 1976

	7:00	7:30	8:00	8:30	9:00	9:30	10:00	10:30
CBS	[......	Local ......]	[... Spencers Pilots ...]		[............ CBS Friday Night Movie ....]			
NBC	[......	Local ......]	Sanford and Son	Chico and the Man	[... Rockford Files ..]		[........ Serpico ......]	
ABC	[......	Local ......]	[.. Donny and Marie .]		[............ ABC Friday Night Movie ....]			

SATURDAY
1976

	7:00	7:30	8:00	8:30	9:00	9:30	10:00	10:30
CBS	[......	Local ......]	The Jeffersons	Doc	Mary Tyler Moore Show	Bob Newhart Show	[	Carol Burnett Show]
NBC	[......	Local ......]	[..... Emergency ....]		[............	NBC Saturday Night Movie	....	]
ABC	[......	Local ......]	Holmes and Yoyo	Mr. T and Tina	[..	Starsky and Hutch]	[...	Most Wanted ....]

SUNDAY
1977

	7:00	7:30	8:00	8:30	9:00	9:30	10:00	10:30
CBS	[....	60 Minutes .....]	Rhoda	On Our Own	All in the Family	Alice	[......	Kojak ....]
NBC	[..........	Wonderful World of Disney	...........]		[..............		Big Event	...........]
ABC	Hardy Boys/Nancy Drew	[...... Mysteries ......]	[Six Million Dollar Man]		[..............	ABC Sunday Night Movie	....	]

MONDAY 1977

	7:00	7:30	8:00	8:30	9:00	9:30	10:00	10:30
CBS	[...... Local ......]		[Young Dan'l Boone]		Betty White Show	Maude	[...... Rafferty ......]	
NBC	[...... Local ......]		[Little House on the Prairie ......]		[............ NBC Monday Night Movie ....]			
ABC	[...... Local ......]		[San Pedro Beach Bums ......]		[............ Sporting Events ....]			

TUESDAY 1977

	7:00	7:30	8:00	8:30	9:00	9:30	10:00	10:30
CBS	[...... Local ......]		[.. The Fitzpatricks .]		M*A*S*H	One Day at a Time	[..... Lou Grant .....]	
NBC	[...... Local ......]		[Richard Pryor Show]		[.. Mulligan's Stew .]		[..... Police Woman ..]	
ABC	[...... Local ......]		Happy Days	Laverne and Shirley	Three's Company	Soap	[...... Family ......]	

WEDNESDAY 1977

	7:00	7:30	8:00	8:30	9:00	9:30	10:00	10:30
CBS	[⋯⋯	Local ⋯⋯]	Good Times	Busting Loose	[⋯⋯⋯⋯	CBS Wednesday Night Movie ⋯⋯⋯⋯		]
NBC	[⋯⋯	Local ⋯⋯]	Life and Times of Grizzly [⋯⋯ Adams ⋯⋯]		[⋯	Oregon Trail ⋯]	[⋯⋯	Big Hawaii ⋯⋯]
ABC	[⋯⋯	Local ⋯⋯]	[⋯	Eight is Enough ⋯]	[⋯	Charlie's Angels ⋯]	[⋯⋯	Baretta ⋯⋯]

THURSDAY 1977

	7:00	7:30	8:00	8:30	9:00	9:30	10:00	10:30
CBS	[⋯⋯	Local ⋯⋯]	[⋯⋯	The Waltons ⋯⋯]	[⋯	Hawaii Five-O ⋯]	[⋯	Barnaby Jones ⋯]
NBC	[⋯⋯	Local ⋯⋯]	[⋯⋯	Chips ⋯⋯]	[⋯	Man from Atlantis]	[⋯	Rosetti and Ryan ⋯]
ABC	[⋯⋯	Local ⋯⋯]	Welcome Back, Kotter	What's Happening!!	Barney Miller	Carter Country	[⋯⋯	Redd Foxx Comedy Hour ⋯⋯]

FRIDAY
1977

	7:00	7:30	8:00	8:30	9:00	9:30	10:00	10:30
CBS	[...... Local ......]		New Adventures of [... Wonder Woman ..]		[... Logan's Run ...]		[...... Switch ......]	
NBC	[...... Local ......]		Sandford Arms	Chico and the Man	[... Rockford Files ...]		[...... Quincy ......]	
ABC	[...... Local ......]		[... Donny and Marie .]		[............ ABC Friday Night Movie ....]			

SATURDAY
1977

	7:00	7:30	8:00	8:30	9:00	9:30	10:00	10:30
CBS	[...... Local ......]		Bob Newhart Show	We've Got Each Other	The Jeffersons	Tony Randall Show	[Carol Burnett Show]	
NBC	[...... Local ......]		[.. Bionic Woman ..]		[............ NBC Saturday Night Movie ....]			
ABC	[...... Local ......]		Fish	Operation Petticoat	[. Starsky and Hutch]		[..... Love Boat .....]	

SUNDAY
1978

	7:00	7:30	8:00	8:30	9:00	9:30	10:00	10:30
CBS	[..... 60 Minutes .....]		[...... Mary ......]		All in the Family	Alice	[........ Kaz ......]	
NBC	Wonderful World of [........ Disney ......]		[...... Big Event ......]				[...... Lifeline ......]	
ABC	[Hardy Boys Mysteries]		[Battlestar Galactica .]		[ABC Sunday Night Movie ....]			

MONDAY
1978

	7:00	7:30	8:00	8:30	9:00	9:30	10:00	10:30
CBS	[...... Local ......]		WKRP in Cincinnati	People	M*A*S*H	One Day at a Time	[..... Lou Grant .....]	
NBC	[...... Local ......]		Little House on the [........ Prairie ......]		[...........] NBC Monday Night Movie			
ABC	[...... Local ......]		Welcome Back, Kotter	Operation Petticoat	[.......... Sporting Events ......]			

TUESDAY
1978

	7:00	7:30	8:00	8:30	9:00	9:30	10:00	10:30
CBS	[........	Local ....]	[....	Paper Chase ....]	[..............	CBS Tuesday Night Movie	....	]
NBC	[........	Local ....]	[....	Grandpa Goes to Washington .....]	[..............	Big Event	....	]
ABC	[........	Local ....]	Happy Days	Laverne and Shirley	Three's Company	Taxi	[. Starsky and Hutch	]

WEDNESDAY
1978

	7:00	7:30	8:00	8:30	9:00	9:30	10:00	10:30
CBS	[........	Local ....]	The Jeffersons	In the Beginning	[..........	CBS Wednesday Night Movie	....	]
NBC	[........	Local ....]	Dick Clark's Live Wednesday .....]	[..........	NBC Wednesday Night Movie	....	]
ABC	[........	Local ....]	[.. Eight Is Enough .]	[.. Charlie's Angels .]	[.......	Vegas	]

THURSDAY
1978

	7:00	7:30	8:00	8:30	9:00	9:30	10:00	10:30
CBS	[......	......]	[....	The Waltons ...]	[..	Hawaii Five-O ..]	[..	Barnaby Jones ..]
NBC	[......	......]	[....	Project U.F.O. ..]	[......	Quincy ......]	[......	W.E.B. ......]
ABC	[......	......]	Mork and Mindy	What's Hap-pening	Barney Miller	Soap	Family ......]	

FRIDAY
1978

	7:00	7:30	8:00	8:30	9:00	9:30	10:00	10:30
CBS	[......	......]	[... New Adventures of	Wonder Woman ..]	[..	Incredible Hulk ..]	[.....	Flying High ...]
NBC	[......	......]	Waverly Wonders	Who's Watching the Kids?	[..	Rockford Files ...]	[Eddie Capra Mysteries]	
ABC	[......	......]	[..	Donny and Marie .]	[.............	ABC Friday Night Movie ....]		

265

SATURDAY 1978

	7:00	7:30	8:00	8:30	9:00	9:30	10:00	10:30
CBS	[...... Local ......]		Rhoda	Good Times	[.. American Girls ..]		[....... Dallas ......]	
NBC	[...... Local ......]		[...... Chips ......]		[...... Specials ......]		[.. Sword of Justice .]	
ABC	[...... Local ......]		Carter Country	Apple Pie	[.. The Love Boat ..]		[.. Fantasy Island ..]	

SUNDAY 1979

	7:00	7:30	8:00	8:30	9:00	9:30	10:00	10:30
CBS	[.... 60 Minutes ....]		Archie Bunker's Place	One Day at a Time	Alice	The Jeffersons	[Trapper John, M.D.]	
NBC	[Disney's Wonderful World ......]		[.............. The Big Event ....]				[Prime Time Sunday ..]	
ABC	Out of the Blue	A New Kind of Family	Mork and Mindy	The Associates	[.............. ABC Sunday Night Movie ....]			

MONDAY 1979

	7:00	7:30	8:00	8:30	9:00	9:30	10:00	10:30
CBS	[.......	Local ....]	[	The White Shadow]	M*A*S*H	WKRP in Cincinnati	[.....	Lou Grant .....]
NBC	[.......	Local ....]	[	Little House on the Prairie ....]	[...........	Monday Night at the Movies ....]		
ABC	[.......	Local ....]	[.....	240–Robert .....]	[...........	Sporting Events ....]		

TUESDAY 1979

	7:00	7:30	8:00	8:30	9:00	9:30	10:00	10:30
CBS	[.......	Local ....]	[..	California Fever .]	[...........	CBS Tuesday Night Movie ....]		
NBC	[.......	Local ....]	The Misadventures of .... Sheriff Lobo ....]		[........	Tuesday Night at the Movies ....]		
ABC	[.......	Local ....]	Happy Days	Angie	Three's Company	Taxi	[......	The Lazarus Syndrome ......]

WEDNESDAY
1979

	7:00	7:30	8:00	8:30	9:00	9:30	10:00	10:30
CBS	[......	Local ......]	The Last Resort	Struck by Lighting	[......	CBS Wednesday Night Movie ......]		
NBC	[......	Local ......]	[......	Real People ...]	Diff'rent Strokes	Hello, Larry	[From Here to Eternity]	
ABC	[......	Local ......]	[... Eight Is Enough .]		[.. Charlie's Angels .]		[...... Vegas ......]	

THURSDAY
1979

	7:00	7:30	8:00	8:30	9:00	9:30	10:00	10:30
CBS	[......	Local ......]	[...	The Waltons ...]	[..	Hawaii Five-O ...]	[...	Barnaby Jones ...]
NBC	[......	Local ......]	Buck Rogers in the 25th Century [......]		[......	Quincy ......]	[...	Kate Columbo ...]
ABC	[......	Local ......]	Laverne and Shirley	Benson	Barney Miller	Soap	[......	20/20 ......]

FRIDAY
1979

	7:00	7:30	8:00	8:30	9:00	9:30	10:00	10:30
CBS	[......	Local ......]	[The Incredible Hulk]		[The Dukes of Hazzard]		[Dallas ......]	
NBC	[......	Local ......]	[......	Shirley ......]	[The Rockford Files]		[......	Eischied ......]
ABC	[......	Local ......]	[.. Fantasy Island ..]		[.............. ABC Friday Night Movie ....]			

SATURDAY
1979

	7:00	7:30	8:00	8:30	9:00	9:30	10:00	10:30
CBS	[......	Local ......]	The Bad News Bears		[.... Big Shamus, Little Shamus ...]		[.........	Paris ......]
NBC	[......	Local ......]	[......	Chips ......]	[.. BJ and the Bear ..]		[.. A Man Called Sloane]	
ABC	[......	Local ......]	The Ropers	Detective School	[.. The Love Boat ..]		[.... Hart to Hart ...]	

SUNDAY
1980

	7:00	7:30	8:00	8:30	9:00	9:30	10:00	10:30
CBS	[..... 60 Minutes .....]		Archie Bunker's Place	One Day at a Time	Alice	The Jeffersons	[Trapper John, M.D.]	
NBC	Disney's Wonderful [........ World ....]		[........ Chips ....]		[............... The Big Event ....]			
ABC	Those Amazing [....... Animals ....]		[.. Charlie's Angels .]		[........... ABC Sunday Night Movie ....]			

MONDAY
1980

	7:00	7:30	8:00	8:30	9:00	9:30	10:00	10:30
CBS	[....... Local ....]		Flo	Ladies Man	M*A*S*H	House Calls	[.... Lou Grant ....]	
NBC	[....... Local ....]		Little House on the [........ Prairie ....]		[...... Monday Night at the Movies ......]			
ABC	[....... Local ....]		[. That's Incredible .]		[........... Sporting Events ....]			

TUESDAY
1980

	7:00	7:30	8:00	8:30	9:00	9:30	10:00	10:30
CBS	[......	Local ......]	[	The White Shadow]	[...........	CBS Tuesday Night Movie ....]		
NBC	[......	Local ......]	[........	Lobo ......]	[........	Harper Valley P.T.A.]	[...	Flamingo Road ...]
ABC	[......	Local ......]	Happy Days	Laverne and Shirley	Three's Company	Too Close for Comfort	[....	Hart to Hart ....]

WEDNESDAY
1980

	7:00	7:30	8:00	8:30	9:00	9:30	10:00	10:30
CBS	[......	Local ......]	[........	Enos ....]	[........	The CBS Wednseday Night Movie ....]		
NBC	[......	Local ......]	[.....	Real People ....]	Diff'rent Strokes	Sanford	[.......	Quincy ....]
ABC	[......	Local ......]	[...	Eight Is Enough .]	Taxi	Soap	[.......	Vegas ....]

272

THURSDAY 1980

	7:00	7:30	8:00	8:30	9:00	9:30	10:00	10:30
CBS	[......	Local ......]	[...	The Waltons ...]	[...	Magnum, P.I. ...]	[...	Knots Landing ..]
NBC	[......	Local ......]	[	Games People Play]	[......	NBC Thursday Night at the Movies ......]		
ABC	[......	Local ......]	[Mork and Mindy	Bosom Buddies	Barney Miller	It's a Living	[......	20/20 ......]

FRIDAY 1980

	7:00	7:30	8:00	8:30	9:00	9:30	10:00	10:30
CBS	[......	Local ......]	[	The Incredible Hulk]	[	The Dukes of Hazzard]	[......	Dallas ......]
NBC	[......	Local ......]	[Here's Boomer	The Facts of Life	[	Speak Up, America .]	[.	NBC News Magazine with David Brinkley]
ABC	[......	Local ......]	[Benson	I'm a Big Girl Now	[......	ABC Friday Night Movie ......]		

273

SATURDAY
1980

	7:00	7:30	8:00	8:30	9:00	9:30	10:00	10:30
CBS	[....... Local ....]		WKRP in Cincinnati	The Tim Conway Show	[Freebie and the Bean]		Secrets of Midland Heights ......]	
NBC	[....... Local ....]		[.... Buck Rogers ...]		[... BJ and the Bear ..]		[... Hill Street Blues .]	
ABC	[....... Local ....]		[.. Breaking Away ..]		[.. The Love Boat ..]		[.. Fantasy Island ..]	

ABOUT THE AUTHOR

Marc Eliot was born in the Bronx in 1946. He graduated from Manhattan's High School of Performing Arts, received a B.A. degree from The City University of New York at City College, an M.F.A. degree of Columbia University's School of the Arts Writing Division, and studied film for two years at the doctoral level, also at Columbia University. He has taught media courses at The City University of New York, Columbia University, and Marymount Manhattan College. His writing has appeared in numerous publications. His first book, *Death of a Rebel*, was a biography of Phil Ochs. Marc has written a prime-time network television special, and has been one of the producer-writers of "The Tomorrow Show." He currently divides his time living in Hollywood, New York City and Palenville, New York. At present he is working on a novel about two Broadway actresses, and a book about discount thinking in Los Angeles.

INDEX

282 INDEX